RECLAIM YO[...] TO GROW OLD

How to immerse yourself in, be curious about,
and celebrate life's most important stage.

KATHLEEN O'BRIEN

To my mother-in-law, Dorothy,
who taught me how to age.

Contents

FOREWORD
(Because you can't go backward.)

I am getting old.

At least that's how I felt as I neared sixty, more than ten years ago. I figured I had two choices: go along with the popular approach to aging and like everybody else, pretend it wasn't happening to me. Or find another way to think about the years ahead.

Aging is inevitable, and I thought maybe we live to be old for a reason.

It turns out we do.

Once I started researching aging and history in detail, I discovered I wasn't the only person who had ever wondered about the meaning of old age. Volumes of wisdom had been written by ancient philosophers, particularly Eastern thinkers. And their interpretation of what later life should be was, by modern standards, radical.

Then science weighed in. I found that forward-thinking gerontologists, anthropologists, and psychologists were diving into everything from the quantification of wisdom to whether old people could "transcend" earthly attachments. The data were giving the scientific community pause about the importance of aging.

My research denouement was startling: both modern science and ancient thinkers shared a similar view of what it means to grow old. And their advice bore little resemblance to what popular culture tells us about how to age.

We are not supposed to deny our old age or fight it. This goes against the natural rhythm of life, both scientifically and philosophically. Instead we should find reassurance in knowing each stage of the human life cycle has a purpose. In our later years we're meant to be more attuned to our inner selves. We're supposed to live our lives with an authenticity and happiness that comes from self-exploration and self-acceptance.

How did our current cultural take on aging, which is all about denying our age or battling against it, become so widespread? Why haven't we heard more about the time-honored splendors of growing old rather than constant admonitions to "stay young?"

There are a number of reasons and **Reclaim Your Right to Grow Old** explores many of them. But our preoccupation with perpetual youth as a goal and the money to be made from more than 76 million baby boomers buying into this mindset certainly play a role.

After teaching classes on my reclaim-your-right-to-grow-old philosophy through the University of Denver's continuing education program, I decided this new, yet centuries-old, blueprint for aging deserved a book.

Throughout the three-and-a-half-year process of putting **Reclaim Your Right to Grow Old** together, I've seen glimmers of ancient wisdom and leading-edge scientific research surface. Famous older people have started using the word *elder*. Pro-aging groups are popping up around the country. Advertisers are beginning to back away from the term *anti-aging*. Most heartening, those in the field of gerontology now talk about a coming paradigm shift that will change how we see our aging selves.

Does this mean the time is right for adopting a transformative way to age? In some ways, timing couldn't be better.

There is an older population that is large enough to encourage real change in how we think about aging. It's just a matter of people finally deciding they don't want to work so hard trying to be something they're not—young again.

There is no going backward. Despite what any cosmetics manufacturer, plastic surgeon, or aging guru tells you, there is no way to stop the aging process. Someday we may slow it down, but we're always going to age. Why wouldn't we want to? Life has moved inexorably forward since we were first part of it, and we've been along for a most adventurous ride.

Didn't we always want to be older when we were kids? Weren't we eager then to know what was next, what was around the corner? That feeling of wanting to know what awaits us is still there. Now that you've put in your time gathering mastery for your later years, the moment has come to pour all that you are into a glorious celebration of elderhood.

As the ancients might remind you, you're only old once.

Kathleen O.

Chapter One
The Best Thing Ever.

Pay no attention to the rest of the world, enamored with wrinkle creams, fighting old age with all their might. They are missing out on the time of their lives.

Because the act of growing old, and everything that goes with it, may be the most important experience you have as a human being. Aging is how you sum up your life. It's how you go deep to the essence of who you are. And the process of getting older can actually make you happy.

This isn't news from outer space. Though if you live in our modern, Western culture, that's how it sounds. Aging with intent and happiness is a philosophy that originated in our own little world, thousands of years ago. It goes back to Eastern and ancient thinkers who have long praised the power of old age.

To reclaim our right to grow old is to understand that aging is natural. Everybody does it. Even the word *elderhood* (a mantle of honor in many enduring societies) is meant to describe a stage of life replete with splendid aspects and roles.

Today, a number of Western gerontologists talk about the

potential of elderhood and the right of older people to immerse themselves in it, but you don't hear enough about their research in mainstream media. What these enlightened scientists say, if you're listening, is that aging is so significant we need to go through it in order to live life to its fullest.

Think for a moment about how far you've come. You've managed to be born and live through childhood and adolescence. You've been educated and gained competence and confidence. You have loved, perhaps married and had children and grandchildren. You have family and friends, and though some of them may be gone, their influence remains in you.

You've been happy, sad, angry, frustrated, relieved, exhilarated, worried, and, at times, at peace. You've experienced almost everything in life except what pulls it all together, what makes life make sense. That's when being older comes in handy. Because now you have the maturity, wisdom and perspective you need to come to some conclusions.

It's lucky you're still around to get old. People feel this way in many Eastern cultures. They even like using the word *old*!

Aging Hindus, for example, don't worry about cellulite, any slow creep of wrinkles, or loosening skin. They're too busy enjoying the last two stages of their lives. There are typically four life stages in the Hindu religion: Youth, when you take the world in. Householder, when you take care of others. Then Elder and Ascetic (it's better than it sounds), when you search for your spiritual self. Hindus believe old age is so momentous they devote *half* the Hindu life cycle to it. Would that we had half their enthusiasm for aging. We could have, if we broke off our love affair with youth and looked at our own elderhood with curiosity, acceptance, and actual anticipation. We need to flip the stereotype of aging on its head and let the rollout of this magnificent time work for us, not against us.

When you fully enter into elderhood, the apex of the human life cycle according to scientists, you turn age to your advantage. You begin to see why this period is exceptional in ways no other part of your life could ever be.

These are the days to fall in love with yourself, do what pleases you, and appreciate who you've become. Now is the time to view your aging body not only with tenderness but admiration. This is the moment to deeply reflect on your life, explore your spirituality, and give the wisdom you've accumulated to younger generations. You can even learn to change your relationship with time, and the inevitable aspect of life no one wants to talk about, death.

It is in your later years that you are supposed to let go of the burdens of middle age and accept the bounty of elder life. That's why it's important to put the focus completely on the older you, not on trying to recapture the younger you who hasn't been seen in years.

At some point you probably thought you *would* be young forever. You may recall the indistinguishable days, one merging with the next, that you spent playing in your back yard as a kid. Or when you were a little older, evenings you'd borrow your parents' car and pick up friends just to cruise around. Going where? It didn't matter. Your time to be young had no end you could see. You didn't give a thought to endings.

What are the chances you can go back and be young again or that you can keep the force of aging at bay? Childhood, adolescence, and, one could argue, adulthood are gone. You have moved on from them to make room for life's capstone. The building stages of the life cycle have given way to your grandest hour, ancient philosophers and scientific research-ers would tell you. If we could summon these academics and sages to sit down with us, these people who have given such careful thought to old age, here's what they might advise:

1. Let go of outward "accomplishment" and go inward to find your true self.
2. Tell people your age. Pretending to be young gets old.
3. Learn to be lazy.
4. Find beauty in the older face, especially your own.
5. Expect young people to respect you. They should.
6. Find happiness in your own eccentricities. Develop more of them if you want.
7. See death as a meaningful and reassuring part of life.
8. Remember, there is a reason we age in the first place. Now you can discover it for yourself.

It can be easier than you think to make peace with the aging process and embark on a different path, one you're ready for only after you've lived a number of decades. You're not lim-ited to your own backyard anymore, you don't have to please your parents or borrow their car. You don't need to look like a million bucks in a bikini. Those were restrictions and pressures you might have had when you were young.

Now you're free for much more important work, and it has nothing to do with combating old age. It has everything to do with being happy with your aging self.

To transform your feelings about getting older and shed a few modern Western prejudices, you may want to head East, the place where many of the foundations of elderhood were laid down. It's here you'll start to appreciate why reclaiming your right to grow old could be one of the best things you ever do.

CHAPTER TWO
You, with a Little Eastern Exposure.

You are sitting on a carved-wood chair. Your feet float in a basin of warm water.

It is 1930s China, and your daughter-in-law is washing your feet. She does this for you, her mother-in-law, out of respect for your importance and seniority. As you sit you are reminded why a certain Chinese maxim has become your favorite: *Great traditions must never be tampered with.*

It is present-day China, and you part the curtains in the living room of your home to see if your children have arrived. You know they'll be here this afternoon because several years earlier China passed a law requiring young people to visit their aging parents and provide for them, which means you, lovely elder, are set for life.

Pencil in mom and dad, kids, because you're going to have to swing by this weekend.

Being an elder Chinese, you find yourself increasingly fond of the legend of Lao-Tzu (or Laozi), a central figure in Taoism. Traditional texts say Lao-Tzu stayed in the womb for sixty-two years. He was born an old man with a gray beard and long earlobes, which are symbols of wisdom and long life. Lao-Tzu literally means "old master." Good to know that *old* is the honorific.

Because you grew up in China you've always been partial to the teachings of Confucius (551—479 BCE), the Chinese philosopher of sweeping influence. He believed the principle of *filial piety* was "the most fundamental of . . . values, the root of all others."

Filial piety is all about younger people respecting their parents and other elders. The Chinese word for this concept is *xiao* and the Chinese character for *xiao* shows a young man holding up an old man.

As an older person raised on ancient traditions, you have an intrinsic understanding of *xiao*, this symbiotic relationship where parents care for children and then children take care of their parents. The point, as anyone in China knows, is that the young are supposed to look after parents when they have reached old age, revere them, and even make sacrifices to them after they have died. No doubt your kids will tamper with the last part of this great tradition.

Meantime, back in the West where most of us don't interact much with Eastern rituals, we may find terms like *namaste* exotic and open to interpretation. *Namaste* is on bumper stickers, and yoga instructors, at the end of class, say it to their students instead of goodbye.

Namaste is Sanskrit and means, "the spirit in me honors the spirit in you" or "I bow to you". But in India young folks make a habit of saying *namaste* to many older people in their lives. They even bow and touch the feet of certain elders— their relatives and teachers—when they greet them.[1]

There's something about being old, cared for, and cared about that resonates, graveside sacrifices and feet-touching aside. How pleasant it would be to live in an environment that values us as we grow older. How different this environment is from the way our modern, Western world treats aging humans.

No one in our world is probably going to bow and say *namaste* as they pass us in the neighborhood. But if *we* think we deserve a *namaste*, or the attention of younger generations because of what we have to offer, we might begin to change our *own* views of our experience and wisdom, and ultimately our importance.

At this point we don't expect people to care for or about us. We're not supposed to be a bother. If we don't value our own needs, though, who will? The need for respect and care begins with us, as many in Eastern cultures will tell you. This is an important step in learning to be happy with the older person we've become.

Here is another:

> *You are sitting cross-legged (if it's comfortable) in the sun, looking out at other mountaintops.*
>
> *You are alone, without self-consciousness. You feel at ease, as if you're part of the warm rock underneath you.*
>
> *You begin to meditate, closing your eyes, breathing in, breathing out.*
>
> *You sit and breathe on your imaginary mountain. After a number of minutes, you open your eyes and bring yourself back from your meditative state, happy to be alone with the living being known as you.*
>
> > *We sit together, the mountain and me, until*
> > *only the mountain remains.*[2] *—Li Po*

You feel rested as if you've been asleep, but you've been quite awake, awake to your breathing and to your older, knowing self.

Meditation, like the illusory mountaintop experience, can be simple and yet have a profound effect on the way you feel about yourself as you age. It is good to see that as you grow older and break free from past responsibility, you will have time to retreat from routine and absorb natural beauty. Whether it is nature's real splendor or part of your mind's passage into meditation (more on this later), both can bring you happiness. Ask an elder in India. And here's the paradox: the less time you have in the scheme of things, West or East, the more time you now have to enjoy it.

Love yourself and be awake—Today, tomorrow and always.

The Buddha

We love what we attend.[3]

Mwalimu Imara

Loving what we attend includes attending to ourselves.

Linger with these thoughts for a few moments, and as with meditation, you can find yourself in a more peaceful place. You may want to come back here after you read the next few pages.

You, with a Lot of Western Angst.

You're no longer on a mountain. Instead you're about to be mowed down by a giant marketing machine, an instrument whose sole purpose is to keep you from feeling good about growing old.

Why No One Wants You to be the Older You. (the short version)

By now it may be obvious what Western society is up to. They don't want you to be yourself, love the older you, or age naturally. What they want is for you to pursue the dream of staying young forever. Why? Because there's a lot of money to be made when you buy into the idea that you can look younger, feel younger, and be younger. When you believe the older you isn't good enough, our appearance-absorbed, youth-bent culture and its marketing apparatus count on you to buy expensive anti-aging potions, cosmetics, and clothes.

They want you to squeeze into tummy-flattening underwear, get wrinkle-reducing injections, hair transplants, plastic surgery, and have your spider veins removed. They're hoping you'll get your teeth capped, hire a personal trainer, buy diet books, and maybe even a sports car.

Lest our cynical side prevails, there is another, much more profound reason Western society doesn't want you to age or even find peace with the aging process. And it's bound up in the core of our Western psyche: we are afraid of growing old.

Why No One Wants You to be the Older You. (the longer version)

Noted academics (I'm not one) have written books on why societies, many of them Western, have had such a contentious relationship with the aging process. Here are some highlights:

It all started with graveyards. Not *all* of it perhaps, but graveyards played a role in how we've come to view aging. According to French philosopher and cultural theorist, Jean Baudrillard, referenced in *The Psychology of Death* by Robert Kastenbaum, ". . . the separation of the dead from the living was one of the most consequential maneuvers in human history."[4] Kastenbaum writes that this separation of the dead into graveyards, rather than burying them in our backyards, became a template for how we came to think about various groups in our society.

People were afraid of the dead and wanted to keep them away from their daily lives. They wanted death literally out of sight. They also weren't too keen on people nearing death or those who lingered on (old people), because old people reminded them that death would ultimately overtake everyone.

How does this "death separation" augur for the older among us? Not well. Unfortunately, we the older are associated with what so many in our Western culture still passionately fear today: their own passing.

The righteous Victorians (the era fashioned by Britain's Queen Victoria from the mid-1800s to early 1900s) were fairly resolute about growing old and dying. Those well-dressed and proper people influenced not only how we viewed the individual in society but how we judged the elderly. Victorian sensibilities persist.

Victorians believed anyone could live a healthy, happy life by simply doing so. If you kept your nose clean, you would live to a very old age, die of natural causes, and head straight for heaven[5]. It was up to you. Never mind diseases caused by genetics, or accidents or mental health issues. Follow God's laws "of morality and health"[6] and you were in like Flynn.

The Victorian view of the world doesn't much help those who struggle with age-related health problems or those who don't "look" like they're aging well. Even today, deep down inside, we may think people who do not have a vigorous old age have somehow been remiss in not living wholesome, healthy lives.

If someone we know "looks old" before her time, we may comment to our spouse, "She's not aging well, is she?" We may feel a certain satisfaction in looking better (or aging more slowly) than our friend. Do we still hold tight to the belief that growing old with mental sharpness and good physical health is under our control?

According to the Health Inequality Project findings of 2019[7], we may have to rethink that. Their study reports that the richest Americans live ten to fifteen years longer than the poorest Americans, and it's not just a matter of access to health care. Poverty itself, the psychosocial impact of being poor, has an effect on longevity. Chronic stress, poor diet, and mental health issues that go unaddressed all contribute to disease and a shorter life. We also have to factor in genetic differences that affect us all.

How much control do we have over how our body physically ages? Can we stop aging or reverse it? Many in the West continue to think we can, and somehow we take solace in that.

No matter what the problem, aging included, we can fix it. Our "can do" American philosophy will not be held back by things like the laws of nature. We *can* stop aging, we tell ourselves. We can make ourselves look younger with plastic surgery. We can reverse the aging process with special concoctions, maybe even stem cells, and never fear, even diseases like cancer can be stopped in their tracks. In a lot of cases they can be, but why do we think the act of growing old needs to be "fixed?" Why are we so sure the fixing can be done?

Here's an unsettling observation. With all the Western medical advances that keep us alive longer, few seem concerned about one of the most powerful inconsistencies of our time: we work hard to help people live longer, but when they do, we cast them aside and ignore them[8]. The old people our advanced civilization helps to age find themselves with no part to play in our advanced civilization.

Maybe an arcane concept called *declinism*[9] can shed light on this.

Declinism, according to William H. Thomas, MD, author of *What Are Old People For?*, is a term used to describe empires that are "past their prime." Past their prime, points out Dr. Thomas, is exactly the way our culture views and describes older people. They are on their way out. They're not useful anymore.

Thomas believes our emphasis on older people's "loss and surrender" over the "miraculous adaptations" people make as they age, is a narrow way to view aging. But this declinist view, he says, is pervasive in our culture. It's about the only way we have to describe what it is to grow old.

> "We have built and continue to enlarge a massive body of knowledge that equates aging with decline and then confidently declares that we decline as we age."[10]

> —William H. Thomas, *What Are Old People For?*

If we think aging signifies only a downward slide (and we do; think of the term *over the hill*), then no wonder we subscribe to the idea that growing old is a grim business. No wonder we want to separate ourselves from it, whether it's to keep ourselves apart from older people in general, or separate ourselves from the older person we are becoming.

Currier and Ives' *Life and Age of Man, Stages of Man's Life from the Cradle to the Grave*, circa 1850, is a perfect example of American declinist thinking[11], though William Thomas wasn't around then to point that out.

The Currier and Ives print shows a series of steps leading to a platform at the top, followed by steps coming down from the platform. On each step is a man in the various stages of his life.

Near the top step is a soldier, climbing to the staircase pinnacle. He has a sword in his hand, is in military costume, and he's sharing the top stair with his slightly older, yet still youthful self. The top of the stairway is not the triumphant man of later years, formed through decades of gaining experience, maturity and wisdom. No, at the apex stands a young, physically robust adult. That's when a man is in his prime, this print says.

The succeeding years, the steps going downward, show the man literally going downhill. At the bottom of the staircase, he is old—bent, useless, forgotten. Is that how people saw themselves then? Is it how we see ourselves now?

Robert N. Butler MD, who founded the National Institutes on Aging, wrote on the first page of his Pulitzer Prize-winning book, *Why Survive?*, "Aging is the neglected step-child of the human life cycle."[12] We can see it in the Currier and Ives print. We can certainly hear Butler's lament in the word *declinism*. We feel it when we look in the mirror and see a face that's growing older. What can we do when society wants us the way we used to be and not the way we are now?

Listen to author Thomas Moore:

> "As I grow older, I feel liberated in many ways, as if my soul is shining more," says Moore (*Care of the Soul*), . . ."I find personal strength in [my] eccentricities and a joy in life that was muffled in earlier years of conformity."[13]

Moore's outlook is like a fresh breeze blowing across the page. Why isn't our Western view of growing older more like his, full of delight, possibility, and even transcendence?

Moore is a former monk, for one thing, so Western pragmatists may consider his take on the world a little woo-woo. But it's also hard for us, no matter how sympathetic we are to Moore and others who embrace aging, to let go of the whole graveyards, Victorian, "can do," *declinism, Stages of Life*, neglected stepchild mindset. It's ingrained in us. And it's going to take a big shift in our thinking about aging to get us closer to a Thomas Moore view of the world. Remarkably, we may be on the cusp of this shift. Like the giant rock plates on the earth's crust that readjust from time to time, our culture is ready to make big adjustments to our take on aging.

I see this desire to shift and resettle into a new aging thought pattern as recapturing ancient and decidedly Eastern ways to age. Western aging experts may see the emerging rearrangement as simply a movement whose time has come. But either way, as you're about to see, timing is everything.

CHAPTER THREE
You, In the Right Place at the Right Time.

How lucky can you be? As we are beginning to grow old, Western gerontologists, psychologists, and academics are beginning to get it. Some thinkers got it more than a century ago, but not a lot of people were paying attention.

Now that the oldest baby boomers are seventy-something, the notion of what it means to age is becoming a hot topic. Status-quo-challenging viewpoints on aging are evolving. They're not widespread, but they are spreading. We're not talking about seventy being the new fifty. If you're seventy and not physically well, hearing that you're supposed to be the "new fifty" may not make you happy.

What we are talking about are Western aging experts who champion what I think is an Eastern and ancient view of aging. Whether you're healthy and active or adjusting to physical issues as you grow older, leaders in gerontology, education, philosophy, and psychology are saying encouraging things.

Some of the good news started way back in 1907. William Graham Sumner presciently wrote in his book *Folkways* that people "in lower civilizations" seem to benefit more from the wisdom of elders than those in "higher civilizations," and younger people "are educated by this experience to respect and value the aged."[1] Sumner's phrasing aside, it appears traditional societies can teach us a thing or two about aging that may be lost on us in our modern, work-a-day world.

In 1922 G. Stanley Hall, psychologist and educator, noted that "modern progress both lengthened old age and drained it of substance."[2] He could already see that though we were living longer, we weren't necessarily happier.

Carl Jung in the 1930s believed "the second half of life should have a very different quality from the first half."[3] It should be a time to look inward and become more reflective. It is also appropriate for older people to be the guarantors of our culture, passing along wisdom and customs to future generations.

Jung said, "A human being would certainly not grow to be seventy or eighty years old if this longevity had no meaning for the species."[4]

Nearing the mid-twentieth century, renowned psychologist Erik Erikson (best known for his eight stages of psychological development) argued that our society's lack of ideal roles for older people means "our civilization does not really harbor a concept of the whole life."[5] How can you have a "whole life," he is saying, if elderhood isn't a meaningful part of it?

But it took Dr. Robert Butler to "put geriatrics on the map," according to Dr. David B. Reuben, chief of the division of geriatrics at the University of California, Los Angeles.[6] Butler, the Pulitzer Prize-winning gerontologist, could rightly be named the father of the new aging paradigm. He began his work later than Erickson, and among other things, articulated a concept called "life review," an almost universal process elders go through as they look back on their past. Researchers believe that life review enables older people to adopt a more sanguine attitude toward their own aging as they grow very old.

Butler also coined the often-tossed-about word *ageism*. He used the term to describe negative stereotyping of older people and what he felt was rampant discrimination against them.

These uncomfortable stereotypes are stubborn. Even today we who are older don't realize how often people invoke them. Terms like *biddy, old goat, codger,* and *cotton heads* rear their heads in our own conversations, and those aren't the worst ones.

Several years ago I started a support group for women entering their later years. We wanted to help each other feel better about our aging selves. I suggested we take one of the stereotyped words used to portray older women and co-opt it.

We decided to call ourselves The Crones and fly in the face of ageism. C.R.O.N.E. is an acronym that stands for Caring, Reflective, Older, Nurturing, Evolving. We affectionately referred to one another with the title *Crone*, as in Crone Kathleen. We flipped the flipping stereotype. I think Butler would've approved.

In his 1975 book, *Why Survive? Being Old in America,* Butler shed light on what I think is a Crone-sanctioned way to approach old age:

> "Human beings need the freedom to live with change, to invent and reinvent themselves a number of times through their lives," he wrote.[7]

Decades ago, Robert Butler planted a seed in our collective consciousness; he raised the issue that aging shouldn't be relegated to an afterthought as we view the expanse of our lives. He said being older has value.

Boy, does it ever, chimed in Maggie Kuhn. In 1970 she moved Butler's philosophy front and center and founded the Gray Panthers. Their aim was to "radicalize a growing number of elderly."[8] Kuhn disliked typical "golden-age clubs," places where aging people were grouped together, calling them "playpens for the old." She declared, "We are not mellow, sweet old people. We have got to effect change, and we have nothing to lose."[9]

Even Ralph Nader jumped in. The activist, and later, presidential candidate, established the Retired Professional Action Group in the early 1970s. He and Robert Butler investigated nursing home practices together.

Almost fifty years ago, a push for a different way to age was underway.

There were obvious reasons for a growing interest in aging,

particularly in the late twentieth century. People were living longer than ever before. There was so much more time to experience life as an older person. So much time to fill with fresh pursuits. How much time? You may be surprised at how short people's lives were, back in the day.

If we were able to time travel to the beginning of recorded history, we would see that most people had barely enough time on earth to reproduce. The average life expectancy in the Cro-Magnon era was eighteen to twenty years. In ancient Rome it was twenty-two. In the Middle Ages people could expect to live into their early thirties.[10] It's true that statisticians have factored in the large number of infant and childhood deaths during these periods, but what we consider today's middle age was their very old age.

In the 1600s William Shakespeare wrote in his second sonnet,

> "When forty winters shall besiege they brow, And dig deep trenches in thy beauty's field. . ."

Shakespeare gives us the sense of how condensed a life could be in the Elizabethan era. A forty-year-old was old. The use of the word "winter" conjures a gray head and fading presence.

Several centuries later, at the beginning of the 1900s in the United States, most people still figured their time was up at about age fifty.[11]

There were people who lived to be sixty or older a couple of thousand years ago, but they were a rare group. Living to ninety was almost inconceivable. It was the increasing use of antibiotics around the time of World War II that gave a big boost to longevity around the world. We're the ones who enjoy the benefits.

The fact that human beings live longer inspired modern-day academics like cultural historian Thomas Cole to delve into the meaning of aging. He says he "hail(s) anyone who is 'playing above the grass,'"[12] meaning he admires any older person who is living and surviving into elderhood and isn't six feet under.

At the same time, Cole warns, we can't expect older people to behave as if they're young adults. As he puts it, our society shouldn't "make it look like if you're sick, it's your own fault; if you're not having orgasms or running marathons, there's something wrong with you."[13] It's okay, he is saying, to live the way you want to as you age. People don't have to "feel like a failure when they can't do the things they used to."[14] That's not what aging is about.

Contemporary philosopher Harry R. Moody has also been on the frontlines of the newest views on aging. In the 1980s he was complaining that the "academic literature of gerontology" was issuing the same advice on growing older as the popular magazines: "keep busy, keep active," as if that's the only road open to older people.[15]

In a 1986 essay, Moody said, "Ancient and medieval civilizations took for granted that the contemplative mode of life represented the highest possibility for human existence."[16]

Today's world favors activity over thoughtfulness, he went on. That doesn't bode well for aging people who are searching for more opportunities to go inward and explore their spiritual side or for people who want to savor their experiences and find deeper fulfillment day to day.

Think about it: if you're an older person and you go to a cocktail party this evening and run into someone you haven't seen in a while, that person will probably start out by asking you, What are you doing these days? Followed by, Keeping busy? They're not going to ask you, What interests you now? What are you thinking about?

These days Harry Moody, who might ask the more thought-provoking questions, edits the *Human Values in Aging Newsletter*, which is distributed electronically by the Gerontological Society of America. After years in high-profile business and academic positions, he now lectures on "conscious aging."

A norm-bucking view of what it means to age, "conscious aging" emphasizes a "holistic path. . . depict[ing] later life as a time for growth of consciousness and wisdom."[17] It is not about success and productivity. It is not about making old age into a second middle age. It is about becoming the person we were meant to be, with greater awareness of ourselves and our place in the cosmos.

Dr. Moody does admit that conscious aging may require more engagement than the conventional roadmap for growing old that stresses accomplishment over contemplation.

But he clearly thinks the effort is worth it. So do I.

Others who are putting their shoulders into moving the aging status quo include powerhouse geriatrician William H. Thomas, MD. (I taught a University of Denver continuing education class through the Osher Lifelong Learning Institute program on Thomas's 2004 book, *What Are Old People For?*)

If you read anything Thomas has written, you find out quickly that he doesn't mince words. He calls adulthood a cult.[18]

He says it is adults (young adults and middle-aged people) who want older people to keep themselves perpetually young. Everyone must conform to "adult" standards—be productive, be busy, strive to succeed. There is no room for the elder in our society. Thomas differentiates between an adult and an elder.

"We are so thoroughly drenched in the doctrine of youth's perfection that we no longer recognize its scent,"[19] says Thomas. We are overpowered by the "action-oriented role that *adults* play in society and history."[20] "Adults think everyone should be an adult no matter how long he or she lives. Nothing else quite measures up."[21] We even want kids to be little adults, he adds.

Is this why we often feel marginalized? As we get older we are no longer young adults or even middle-aged ones. So we think we no longer fit in?

A friend of mine was in New York City recently at a swanky art gallery. She was asked if she wanted a senior ticket for the event. She hesitated because, although she's senior by age, she always believed she looked younger than her years. She thought, Does this mean I have a special designation now? Do I no longer look like the hip, young people going in the door? Do I need a senior ticket because I am an old woman?

I have to add, my friend is open-minded about aging. But at that moment, she felt like she was back in high school, hoping to be part of the in-crowd instead of being grouped with the less-than-cool. That is, the old folks.

This is what William Thomas is describing. We don't realize how adult-oriented our society is until we're told we're not one of the adults anymore.

In no uncertain terms, Thomas is out to change people's thinking about what it means to age. As a professor at the University of Maryland's Erickson School and the president of the global nonprofit The Eden Alternative, Thomas speaks out regularly on aging issues worldwide.

There are many others who are on a mission to help you age the way you were meant to, to free you from aging stereotypes and your own sometimes self-defeating take on growing old, so you can blossom in what some academics call "the third age."

People rooting you on range from the late Rabbi Zalman

Schachter-Shalomi who authored *From Age-Ing to Sage-Ing: A Profound New Vision for Growing Older*, to twenty-nine-year-old Amanda Cavaleri, who heads a nonprofit headquartered in Denver geared to bringing young people into geriatric fields.

Do you remember when people used to smoke in elevators and on airplanes? When men had "one for the road" and thought it was fine to drink and drive? Remember when women covered up their pregnancies in big smocks with bows at the neck and referred to themselves as "in a family way"? Lots of things have changed in a relatively short amount of time. It's not much of a stretch to think we can change the way we view aging too. Being in the right place at the right time is almost enough to keep the momentum going. It's almost enough to have your hand on a door that is opening to an inventive way of thinking about your aging self and the rest of your life.

Here's where some inspiration may be helpful:

As I age, may I be kind to myself.

It's a line from the Loving Kindness aspiration prayer.[22] Everything about changing our culture's take on growing older, everything about how we feel about aging and about ourselves may boil down to this sentiment.

It requires us to appreciate the years we've lived. Care about ourselves. Love and forgive ourselves. Put our needs, not second to everyone else's, but squarely in front of us, where they can be seen by us and others. We can do it for ourselves the way we've done it for those around us for so many years.

If you're ready to let go of everyone's expectations and truly be kind to the older you, you will begin your own paradigm shift and open the door to elderhood yourself.

Chapter Four
How You Age is a Choice.

People tell you to age gracefully. It's almost amusing. The advice in our Western culture is either pretend to be younger than you are, or if you must grow old, at least do it with aplomb.

If you're trying to nurture a loving approach toward your aging self, though, where does the idea of aging gracefully fit in?

It doesn't.

Telling older people to age gracefully implies that there is something inherently wrong with aging. You don't ask a child to be a child gracefully, yet older people are supposed to tiptoe around their later years as if growing old is some ignoble exercise.

If you feel you have to age with grace, your later years may become an act to please other people, not to satisfy yourself. You're conforming to the way you think older people should behave.

Aging doesn't have to take effort, either to make yourself appear younger or to be "graceful" as you grow older. Aging comes upon us naturally, and we can wrap the years around us and wear them in any way that suits us.

Is anything expected of us if we want to age with true affection for this older person we are becoming? Is there something we can do to bring the sweet mix of significance, wonder, and reward to the process of growing old?

First of all, we don't have to *do* anything; not in the sense of doing certain things to satisfy a set of goals, as our Western culture usually expects of us.

If we want to reclaim our right to age with happiness, we may want to think about the wisdom the Dalai Lama outlined in his book *The Art of Happiness*:

> *".....the purpose of life is to seek happiness...And as we begin to identify the factors that lead to a happier life, we will learn how ...happiness offers benefits not only for the individual but for the ...family and society at large..."[1]*

My Aunt Mimi, who died a week short of her hundredth birthday, found the Dalai Lama's writing compelling. When she was ninety-nine she told me she wished she had read his books when she was younger. She was rather surprised to discover the purpose of life was to be happy. "Would that I had learned that when I was in my eighties", my aunt said and then laughed. Would that she had.

If we decide our purpose as we grow older is to be happy and feel rewarded for our years, what should our path be?

Perhaps Carl Jung can give us some guidance.

> "For a young person it is almost a sin, or at least a danger, to be too preoccupied with himself; but for the ageing person it is a duty and a necessity to devote serious attention to himself."

He goes on, poetically,

> "After having lavished its light upon the world, the sun withdraws its rays in order to illuminate itself."[2]

Then it's supposed to be all about you? Yes. All about loving and tending to yourself. It is precisely because you have some years behind you, because you have garnered knowledge and have a bigger-picture view of the world, that you can make it about you, that you can turn your attention inward.

In the past the study of ancient Jewish mysticism known as Kabbalah was reserved for people over forty. Much as Jung talked about the "sin" of being self-absorbed, it was considered somewhat dangerous for younger people to take the Jewish mystical journey without having the maturity to appreciate and understand it.

Certain privileges are reserved for age. You must be twenty-one to drink alcohol and thirty-five to be president. Following the erstwhile rules of Kabbalah, you had to reach a specific age to have the privilege of studying mysticism.

Because of our older age now, we have license to concentrate on ourselves. Gerontology professor Robert C. Atchley wrote in *The Inner Work of Eldering*, ". . .the more often people practice being wise, the more likely they are to be able to find that place within themselves from which wisdom comes."[3]

Reflecting on our lives, looking inward to what we've learned and how we can make ourselves happier, is one of the great perquisites of old age.

Here is what Ram Dass says about the Indian view of aging compared to our Western approach:

". . .the old in India enjoy a peace, after the storm of youth, that is largely unknown to aging Americans."

He continues,

"Old age offers the opportunity to shift our cares away from the physical toward what cannot be taken away: our wisdom and the love we offer to those around us."[4]

While we worry about facelifts and erectile dysfunction, the Indian culture encourages people to find peace in their later years. Is it wrong, then, to care about how you look or your sex life? Not at all. But if our focus is only on maintaining our youthful, physical selves, then the stress that goes with trying to stay young may make it more difficult for us to be happy.

What about people who are still working in their mid to late sixties and into their seventies or even eighties? Is it possible for them to work and still find peace as they age? What if they must to work to keep money coming in?

The idea of work and elderhood may not sound compatible. If the purpose of the elder is to concentrate on the inner self, to give wisdom to other generations, to love and nurture those around us, and to be happy, it sounds like work could get in the way.

But if your work draws on your most prized abilities, if it stirs up your passions and offers that fine balance between challenge and enjoyable routine, maybe the job is worth keeping.

What if you are working at a job that makes you unhappy, a job that wears you down? Then it may be time to reevaluate your reasons for getting on the freeway every morning. Oh, I know. You think you need a certain amount of money to get by, you want to contribute to your daughter's education, you'd like to pay off your mortgage.

But have these aspirations become burdens? Have these burdens become more important than moments of real happiness for you?

You don't want to be destitute, but maybe you could get by on less. Could your daughter share more of the burden of her education? Could you find a smaller place to live? Is there a job out there that would allow you more freedom, a job with fewer hours? How about working at something that would be more fun, with a lot less responsibility?

Life is finite, and that fact probably hasn't passed you by.

What are you giving up to continue working at a job you've grown tired of?

David Sanders, director of Kabbalah Experience in Denver tells this story:

> An orthodox Jewish man is in prison, and once a year he is let out for a day of freedom. He worries about what day he should pick to leave the prison for twenty-four hours. Should it be one of the Jewish holidays? Yom Kippur? Rosh Hashanah? Passover? Should it be his birthday? A parent's birthday?

> He decides to write to his rabbi for advice. "When should I leave prison for my day off?" he asks.

> The rabbi writes back one word: "Now."

When you continue to do what you don't want to do or work at a job you no longer enjoy, you're giving up "now". And there is no way in the world to get precious "now" moments back. If you want to make a change in your life, there is no better time than the present.

A couple of years ago in a class I was teaching on aging, Harry, a man a little older than I was, shared his feelings about his struggle to retire:

> "I just don't know if I can do it. My whole life is tied up in my practice (he was a child therapist). If I'm not working, who am I? Besides, I need to keep busy."

In our class we talked about elderhood as a unique and special time to grow in ways we might not have imagined when we were younger. Harry felt he wanted to retire, but something was keeping him from letting go of his work.

About a year later, Harry walked through the door of another class I was teaching. I recognized him, but he looked different. There was something about his face that made him seem more accessible. His features were softer. He was relaxed, and at the same time, engaged.

He told me he had retired and that it was one of the best decisions he had ever made. He was taking camping trips, studying astronomy, delving into his spirituality, reflecting on his life, and spending time with his grandchildren.

He said what had kept him from retiring earlier was the sense that his job was his essence. Being a therapist gave him a role to play and a standing in the world. Harry said he was worried about giving up who he thought he was. He also said he was afraid to admit to himself that he was getting older. But he was pleasantly surprised to find out his worth wasn't tied up in being a therapist. Now Harry has begun a joyous exploration into who else he can be.

Some wisdom from *The Tibetan Book of Living and Dying:*

> Although we have been made to believe that if we let go we will end up with nothing, life itself reveals again and again the opposite: that letting go is the path to real freedom.[5]

It is counterintuitive. The more we let go, the more we gain control. The more we stop striving to live up to some ideal of ourselves, the more we become ourselves.

For years Beth worked as a middle school teacher. After she retired she decided she wanted a life that was more adventurous. So she sold a lot of her things and rented a studio apartment.

Then she started to travel. When she wasn't traveling, she offered her services as a house and pet sitter. Her rent was cheap, so she was able to keep her small place and still be free to take up in someone's home to house sit or journey off on a trip. She ended up selling her car and now gets around by bus, on her bike, or by taking Uber.

Beth says having fewer things is freeing. Without possessions to worry about, she is able to concentrate on what she wants from retirement. "I have never felt more right about myself or my life," she says. That's the idea.

Sam is an artist whose work appears in several museums. After selling his graphic design business twenty-five years ago, he decided he wanted to move from the Midwest to the West Coast, even though he didn't know anyone there. He settled in Los Angeles, then moved to Portland, Oregon.

He's a photographer, painter, and sculptor. Sam has also ventured into acting, singing, and illustrating children's books. He has an almost child-like enthusiasm for starting new projects. "These projects are what keep me going," he says.

His life is simple. He is not hesitant to tell you that he lives on Social Security. "I've outlived most of my savings," he says, "but it doesn't keep me from enjoying my time, my art."

Now Sam is working on a painting for an alumni exhibit at his former art school. He is eighty-five, and despite a number of losses in his life, he describes himself as happy.

You can make a choice about how you want to age. Like Harry or Beth or Sam, you can let go of what our culture wants for you or what you think you're supposed to want for yourself. You can gain control of your later years. When you choose to accept the older you, then pour your love, respect, and nurture into the older person you've become, you're open to all the experiences you were meant to have. And you may find they have nothing to do with aging gracefully.

❮ Scribble *some notes while we're on the subject.* **❯**

How do you see yourself as you age? Visualize you in a snapshot.

Are you hiking in the woods? Meditating? Painting in your own little studio? Traveling to Sri Lanka? Are you taking your grandchildren to the zoo? Are you still working, but at a job you love? Perhaps you're involved in all these things. What kind of elderhood do *you* choose?

Why don't people ever ask us what we want to be when we grow old?

CHAPTER FIVE
Following Your Heart's Desires.

A poem should not mean, but be.

Archibald MacLeish

What do you want to be when you grow up? We often ask our children that question. You can be anything, we say, encouraging them to consider all possibilities as they go through life.

Notice the word we use when we talk to children about roles they can eventually take on: *be.* You can *be* anything.

Using the *be* word means we're smarter than we think, because there is a difference between what our children imagine themselves being and what, as adults, they might describe themselves *doing.* According to William Thomas in *What Are Old People For?*, the difference is crucial.

> "Simple observation has led me to see life as the dynamic and unfolding interplay between the states of doing and being."[1]

What does he mean by *doing* and *being*? In this case, he's talking about the difference between working at something or becoming passionately immersed in it.

To put it another way, if you want to be kind to your aging self and explore what it means to follow your heart's desires, you want to be rather than do.

"*Doing* is what happens when we come into relationship with . . .the. . . material world that surrounds us. Human work is usually thought of in terms of doing," explains Thomas.[2]

Being, says Thomas, is more about the relationship you have with yourself, "who you were, who you are, and who you will become."[3]

"We find meaning in being," he tells us.[4]

Meaning is what we want for our children, and isn't it what we want for ourselves?

Maybe we experienced *being* in the careers we chose, or maybe we were just doing the work. But in our later years, when we have the time to explore our enthusiasms, *being* has allure, just as taking on a role has to a child.

If we truly want to *be*, then how do we go about that? How will *being* rather than *doing* lead us to a happier elderhood?

Your labors in the kitchen may hold some insight:

Think how many times over the years you've said these words to your spouse or children: "I'm going to cook dinner." Which meant you would get out the ingredients, go to the stove, cook something, and then put it on the table.

What if six o'clock rolled around this evening, and instead you said, "Tonight I'm going to be a cook!" What a difference it makes to alter the words ever so slightly. In the first sentence you were going to cook. In the second sentence, you are going to *be* a cook. What does that say about your intention?

Being a cook means you are going to adopt a role. You are going to transform yourself into a chef for the evening. You'll tinker with ingredients, make a gorgeous sauce, and use your imagination putting together a special meal.

You are going to have fun.

When your approach to life is to *be* rather than *do*, that act, deciding to *be*, allows you to live more fully in every moment, to expand each moment into countless offerings, and, like a child playing, fall into a timeless space where you become your role and your role becomes you.

When I sat down to write this book, I decided to think of myself as being a writer. You know, a person with a glass of bourbon on the table, bent over an Underwood. This approach only works in movies.

The concept of *being* a writer meant that I wasn't just sitting down to write. I was taking on a role, one that I had visualized in my mind (which, by the way, didn't have much to do with bourbon unless it was after five o'clock).

The role itself gave me a certain confidence. By its very nature, stepping into the role of a writer assumed that I had the skills to write. Reminding myself of my role kept me going.

Being a writer means it's okay for me to spend the hours it takes to complete a book, to practice over and again putting words together. When I am being a writer, I join into a process of creating. Sometimes it seems what I'm creating takes over, which is often unexpected.

It brings these words to mind:

> *You cannot travel the path*
> *until you have become the path itself.*
>
>   The Buddha

Teacher, poet and potter M.C. Richards describes her early years in what can only be interpreted as a state of *being*:

> "In childhood, the future stood before me like a fairy city of splendors and joys . . . everything shone with improbability and magic. So this is going to school. So this is growing up. So this is knowledge."[5]

M. C. Richards is *being* a child in the truest sense. She encounters the moments in her young life as they come, with appreciation and fascination. So this is going to school, she thinks, as she's experiencing it.

This sense of embrace and discovery is not reserved for children. As older people, we can know these same feelings in our own *being* state. Life can still shine with improbability and magic. In fact, this may be the best time to encounter life's surprising charms. Now we have the maturity to deeply contemplate them, put them into context, and even understand them.

So this is what it's like to be a gardener. You're not here merely to pull weeds; you're here to take in the smell and feel of earth and flowers. To look at the bright shoots on plants with a knowing about how they got here, and a familiar appreciation of how they grow so quickly.

As a gardener you have the skills to enhance your flowers' blooms and an awareness of how the mix of colors you so carefully selected shows off each plant to its advantage. You find your garden to be a peaceful spot, and when you're here it's as if time retreats, and you don't have to make an effort to do anything except marvelously drift in the present.

Being a gardener is like being a writer, a musician, a painter, or a cook. There is a feeling of unfolding mystery along with an assurance that what is not yet known will pull you in and also be welcome.

You are in a most pleasant groove that takes you where you want to go.

So this is *flow*.

THE PARADISE OF FLOW

Ah, *flow*. It's like planting palm trees in your brain, calling up temperate breezes when you like, and digging imaginary toes in the sand. It is a beautiful place where time becomes irrelevant. It's all in your head, but also outside of it. What is this amorphous-sounding thing called *flow*?

I'll let psychologist Mihaly Csikszentmihalyi, who named the concept, describe it to you.

> *[It is] the state in which people are so involved in an activity that nothing else seems to matter.*

He elaborates,

> *. . .the experience is so enjoyable that people will do it even at great cost, for the sheer sake of doing it. . .*[6]

It is, as Csikszentmihalyi's book *Flow* says in its subtitle: The psychology of optimal experience. Well, we certainly want optimal experience as we age, so what's the nitty gritty of *flow*? How does it work, and how can we get in on it?

If you have ever entered the state of *being* for any length of time, you have probably experienced *flow*. When you are being a gardener, a cook or writer, when you're being a hiker in the mountains or a surfer in the ocean, you may have become one with what you were experiencing. You may have felt you never wanted what you were being to stop. You may have lost all track of time. Pulling yourself away from what you were being may have been difficult, even uncomfortable. This is *flow*.

While it sounds like something totally spontaneous and

unconscious, accompanied by unexpected, even random thinking, Csikszentmihalyi says it's the opposite:

> "The optimal state of inner experience is one in which there is *order in consciousness*."[7] And he says, "This happens when . . .attention. . . is invested in realistic goals and when skills match the opportunities for action."[8]

The elation we feel, it turns out, comes from a grounded place. When we choose to *be*, we also can choose to be in the *flow*. In his research, Csikszentmihalyi found that people explained their state of mind as one "when consciousness is harmoniously ordered," and when people want to pursue things for no other reason than the joy of pursuing them.

It's interesting that Csikszentmihalyi talks about realistic goals and our skills matching opportunities for action. For the most part we do gravitate toward activities that offer us reachable satisfaction. If you're not good at math, you probably won't want to be an accountant. If you're a novice painter, you'll probably be happy with modest accomplishments; you won't expect your work to be hung in a museum. At least not right away.

As we grow older, there may be many states of being we want to take on because we think we'll enjoy them and because we have or think we can gain the levels of mastery to handle them.

These objectives may be as sophisticated as studying astronomy like my friend Harry, in the last chapter. Or they may be as simple as playing with your grandchild. When you are *being* a student, *being* a grandparent, and following your heart's desires, you are probably going to be good at what you've decided to be. You will make the effort to be good at it, even though it will seem effortless. And you will have a very nice shot at creating *flow* in your own little paradise.

Sometimes I think *flow* can come from the most mundane activities. I remember being in fifth grade, and our art teacher, Miss Switzer, asked my best friend, Debby, and me to help her take supplies back to the art closet. Everybody loved Miss Switzer, and we felt special because she'd chosen us.

The closet was actually a little windowless room with all kinds of colorful materials and creativity-inducing objects. As we were putting things away, she said we could unpack and organize a few boxes that were sitting on the floor.

After Miss Switzer left, we lost track of time. That Friday afternoon Debby and I spent what might have been several hours rearranging art supplies and tidying up. We wanted the closet to be perfect. We gave no thought to going back to our classroom.

Our fifth-grade teacher was none too happy about our escape, even though we had the best of intentions. Back in the 1950s, kids had to account for their time outside of class, and not many excuses were accepted. Forgetting to tell your teacher where you were wasn't going to fly.

I can't remember if we had to stay after school to atone for our hours of *flow*, but the memory of playing in that art closet stays with me as one of my happiest school experiences. I was lost in a Marie Kondo fantasy.

Little did I know that putting things in their place would be something I would enjoy throughout my life. I can get caught up rearranging kitchen cabinets, the plants in my house, or décor items that I think must be shuffled around from time to time. These tasks may be ordinary, but I still feel the *flow* in them.

". . .if we just act in each moment with composure and mindfulness, each minute of our life is a work of art"

"If we just act with awareness and integrity, our art will flower. . ."[9]

Thich Nhat Hanh
Peace is Every Step

❮ **Jot** *down your thoughts while they're flowing out.* ❯

How often do you let yourself get into a state of *being*?

Think about some of the activities you're doing that could be transformed into moments of *being*. Even your every-day routines. How can you let go more often and just *be*?

Try to recall instances in your life when you've experienced a timeless feeling of joy. What was that like for you? What were you *being* at the time? Make some notes.

Are there some simple ways you can practice living moment to moment? Maybe take a half hour out of your day and try not to think about the past or future. Think only about what you're involved in right now. Focus on the person you're with or the matter at hand. Don't check your phone. Be present. Reflect on how you feel afterward. What's it like to live only in the now? Are you more relaxed, more energized, less stressed?

Now let go and be present in another moment:

> *You are on a bluff, overlooking the ocean. You are being an observer.*
>
> *You have nothing to do but watch the waves. Tiny shards of sunlight shimmer on the surface of the water.*
>
> *You can hear the waves below, the ocean's breath, coming in and going out, like your own breath.*
>
> *You close your eyes and see the ocean.*
>
> *You are part of its rhythm of life as you meditate, high on your imaginary bluff, following your breath.*

After several minutes you slowly bring yourself back from your respite. You are here again, reading this book. You feel relaxed after your brief, spontaneous meditation. You don't have the need to do anything. Which is good because you're about to take another little vacation and cram a week's worth of elation, and most likely *flow,* into one short, remarkable day.

CHAPTER SIX
Would It Kill You to Take a Day Off?

You step out your front door in the morning chill. The sun is beginning to overtake gray shadows. You pick up your paper off the front porch, but you don't want to go back inside.

You want to stay with the morning's newness. Just for a moment, you want to go with it. You allow your mind to explore this possibility. As the sun rises over the trees, you wish you could follow it and let the new day take you where it will. You think about having a day unencumbered by expectations—you, simply floating along with the sun. What if you were to step off the porch and enter this vision in your mind, a kind of endless day?

Have you ever experienced an "endless" day? A day with no obligations, no constraints, one that seems limitless, timeless? Where you get up in the morning and nothing interferes with your pursuit of delight?

Are you out of your mind? you're thinking. No one has days like that.

Oh yes, they do.

Some Eastern cultures have a history of infusing their days

with timelessness, joy, even idleness. Tibet's, among others, comes to mind. One Tibetan woman summed up her culture's affection for doing nothing this way: "We just make a little bit of money and are satisfied and think about having a good time. "[1] Tibetan indulgence in indolence occurs more often than not, according to some who are critical of it.[2]

Though days of being aimlessly idle may seem at odds with our Western habits, we could learn something from people who put their own happiness first. And we can learn a lot from, and perhaps more readily accept, religious groups that celebrate a weekly day off.

For those who observe a Sabbath (Christians, Jews, Muslims, and other spiritual followers), it is a time completely removed from toil and commonplace responsibilities. It is often described by adherents as a day of bliss. Dan Allender, the author of *Sabbath* (from the *Ancient Practices* series), describes this special day of renewal:

> The Sabbath is an invitation to enter delight. . .the best day of our lives.[3]

> The only parameter to guide our Sabbath is delight.
> Will this be merely a break or a joy?[4]

The Sabbath marked by Jews begins on Friday night at sundown. Candles are lit and prayers are said. Family and friends gather for a celebration dinner. While the Jewish Sabbath can have some solemnity to it, it is also a time to enjoy the people around you. The Sabbath meal includes wine, the traditional challah (a rich, braided egg bread, pronounced "ha'-lah,"), and lots of talking, laughing, and even singing.

As the Sabbath extends into Saturday, no thought is given to anything but rest and happiness. Observant Jews attend religious services and honor their faith in other ways, but the point for anyone immersing herself in a Sabbath is to take pleasure from each moment of this special day.

What are we missing here? Other cultures and certain religious groups seem to find the idea of a day (or more) detached from busyness most acceptable, and among some who are devoutly religious, even mandatory. But it is hard for our secular, Western consciousness to embrace the concept of indulging in a day of elation for its own sake.

If you're retired, you may be taking more vacations. But do you allow yourself to get into an "endless day" frame of mind? Do you let yourself partake of the timeless rhythm that is characteristic of a Sabbath and part of the stream of life in some Eastern cultures?

The concept of removing yourself from the cares of daily life and rejoicing in being in the present is ancient. The Jewish Sabbath is enshrined in the Ten Commandments, and honoring God is only part of its intent.

Sabbath rest creates a "sanctuary in time."[5]

Hasidic Rabbi Zalman Schachter describes his vision of Sabbath beauty this way:

". . .the haven of Shabbos [the Sabbath] in the bosom of an unhassling family. . .eating, resting, singing, loving. . . The Sabbath is long and full when one knows how to be beyond doing."[6]

Is the good rabbi talking about "being" instead of "doing?" Tilden Edwards in his book, *Sabbath Time*, says that Sabbath rest involves two stages: "letting go" and being.

Right now you may be thinking this is all fine and good for orthodox religious folks, but I'm not religious, so how can I celebrate a Sabbath? How can I get into the drift of an "endless day" just by letting go and being?

Enter the secular Sabbath. It's an idea that's been popping up in Internet posts for several years. Mark Bittman, former *New York Times* columnist, wrote an article on what he called a "secular Sabbath" back in 2008. [7] (That is, a day of rest with no religious meaning or rituals.) Bittman talked about the difficulty in closing his computer, putting down his cell phone for a day, and distancing himself from work.

A secular Sabbath can be more than eschewing Internet connections, though. It is shutting out the buzz of the world and allowing yourself a day off from life.

What does this mean exactly?

It can mean not only turning off the computer, putting your cell phone on silent mode, and not answering your land line unless it's an emergency (you can tell your relatives about your secular Sabbath ahead of time). But you can also decide not to shop, not to drive, or not to watch TV, unless these things are your earthly form of rapture.

Then let your mind ramble across a list of possible activities or non-activities that would make you happy on your day of leisure. As the sun comes up, would you like to go for a hike? Would you like to lie on a beach? Would you like to read? Try out a new recipe? Do you want to play the piano, draw, go to the museum, have friends in for dinner? Do you want to write an old friend a letter, or just take a nice, long afternoon nap?

Sabbath author, Dan Allender, asks us,

> What would I do for a twenty-four-hour period of time if the only criteria were to pursue my deepest joy?[8]

Maybe you just want to spend time with your family. But the idea is not to feel like you're living up to certain responsibilities. If you want to babysit grandchildren, that's okay, but make sure it's something that, on this day, would make you truly happy. If you want to attend a function, that's fine too. But remember to be honest: Is this an obligation or something I'm looking forward to?

You know how you feel on vacation? I know, Americans are terrible about taking vacations. Many of us never use up our allotted time off each year to rest or to see our own lives from a fresh point of view.

When we're on vacation, though, particularly when we're

traveling, we do get to look at our lives with some perspective. We can observe what we do day-to-day from a physical distance and evaluate how satisfying our life is. Or isn't.

When we devote a day to a secular Sabbath we have the opportunity to look at who we are in a similar way. We can reflect on our circumstances and, released from interruptions and heartened by the peacefulness of our break, take their measure. If we want to make changes, Sabbath moments can give us the encouragement we may need.

Like returning from a good vacation, we can then set in motion our real dreams for ourselves. When we slow down to take in the meaning of our lives, we have renewed zest for speeding up our own transformations.

Slowing down physically is also part of a meaningful secular Sabbath. It's okay to take your time, or even be idle. In his 2013 New York Times Sunday Review article titled "A Stroll Around the World," Paul Salopek talks about his goal of walking 21,000 miles across our earth. On the Gulf of Aqaba in Jordan, he posts this:

> "And then there is simply the act of traveling through the world at three miles an hour—the speed at which we were biologically designed to move. There is something mesmerizing about this pace that I still can't adequately describe."[9]

Taking a walk on your day of play is a good way to see the world anew. We were meant to travel as walkers, not drivers of cars on crowded freeways. What a refreshing way to view our neighborhoods and ourselves if we slow down to three miles an hour.

A secular Sabbath is also a fine time to practice the art of non-consumption. In her book *Soul and the* City, author, poet and academic Marcy Heidish references Rebecca Parker about abstaining from shopping on your day of pleasure:

> Celebrating a Sabbath "is an act of saying no to the message that tells us to fill the emptiness in our lives by consuming more."

> When we take a day off from consuming, "we take a degree of control back in our lives."[10]

They do not pass the collection plate in Jewish synagogues. It is not a day to think about money. Paying for anything, even a religious service, can distract you from your spiritual self.

Let's face it, any time we buy something, we become tethered to it. We have to find a place for this thing we buy. We have to take care of it. When we don't spend money, even for one day, we are refusing the responsibility of owning something new, which frees us up to be in whatever happy moment comes our way.

If you opt to go to the theater on your day of rest, you may have to pay for a ticket at the box office. But if you decide you're not going to spend money on your day off, you can always buy the ticket ahead of time. Or you can decide the ticket is the one exception you'll make to letting go of the obligation to pay.

How hard is it to keep a secular Sabbath? Can people do this week after week? Marcy Heidish writes, "I fail often. Sabbath keeping is a challenge for all of us . . . especially where stores and entertainment and restaurants are open 24/7 and a high level of stimuli, without pause, comes at us."[11]

Dan Allender, from *Sabbath*:

> "The Sabbath is like every other gift—it requires practice and discipline to grow in delight"[12]

Tilden Edwards from *Sabbath Time*:

> Each of us must find our own way to celebrate a Sabbath "through our own discernment and experimental process."[13]

But it can be done. Even if we start with a mini-Sabbath, say just a few hours every weekend, we can find that restful place for ourselves. You can turn off your computer and your phone. You can stop texting, emailing, Instagramming, tweeting, Facebooking, TikTok-ing, Pinteresting, downloading, and using apps. You don't have to be in touch 24/7. It's not going to kill you.

It may help you live longer.

In a *New York Times* article about the long-lived people on the Greek island of Ikaria, Dan Buettner (author of *The Blue*

Zones: Lessons for Living Longer from the People Who've Lived the Longest) interviews one of Ikaria's few physicians who describes life on Ikaria like this: "We wake up late and always take naps. . . Have you noticed that no one wears a watch here?. . .We simply don't care about the clock."[14]

Not caring about the clock is the hallmark of a secular Sabbath. As Ram Dass puts it in his book, *Still Here*:

> "Being time-bound, we're mostly blinded by what is unfolding every moment; we measure and shrink and define these wonders, but when we stop counting, and open our eyes, a new sort of life awaits us."[15]

If you are being kind to your older self and in the process of learning to love the aging you, one of the great gifts you can give yourself is the pleasure of taking a day off. Completely. So you can be in the moment with what gives you contentment. So you can be that contentment.

When I lived in Los Angeles there was a billboard I used to pass every day. It was an ad for a health club that showed a young woman sweating it out in a spin class. The headline read: You Can Rest When You Die.

I'm here to tell you, you don't have to wait that long. You can take one day a week, one afternoon a week, if you'd like, and fill your moments to the brim with what makes you happy. You can rest and rejoice in a space where the day evolves and you tag along.

"I don't need to schedule every minute—birds don't have schedules, why should I?[16]

Ram Dass, *Still Here*

Now that you're old enough to appreciate what you've done during your time as a Householder (as Hindus call the young and middle-aged), you've earned the right to sit back. It doesn't matter how you observe a secular Sabbath as long as you celebrate one exquisite day, or even one afternoon. Okay, try a couple of hours. Start by throwing the clock out the window. Then, like a bird, let the day lift you up and carry you away.

❮ Pencil *in some time that is timeless.* ❯

What day of the week would be best for you to take a vacation from life? If you could step off your front porch and be swept into a few enchanted hours, what would that entail?

Think about putting a date on your calendar for your first secular Sabbath and then fantasize about it below.

This is life at its most sublime. Where could our narrative possibly go from here? Most likely, to the ridiculous.

Chapter Seven
Feeling Ridiculously Good in Your Own Skin.

How old are you? Don't be ridiculous, I'm not answering that question. Is that what you want to say when the subject of your age comes up? You get an uneasy feeling, and you either want to come back with a smart reply or say nothing at all.

At this point in your life, though, you should be shouting your age from the rooftops. Then everybody will know how old I am, you're thinking. That's the idea. When you tell your age, you're revealing something important about yourself. You're telling people who you really are.

You're saying you've lived long enough to know something about life. You've been part of history. You are mature, you have perspective and experience. You are wise. Or if you must, look at it this way: would you rather be an okay-looking fifty-year-old or a fabulous-looking seventy-year-old?

I remember getting carded when I was in my forties. I did not get a kick out of having to show my driver's license to buy a bottle of wine. I was annoyed that someone thought I could possibly be nineteen or twenty. Didn't I dress like someone with maturity? Didn't I look like I had more confidence than a college kid? Didn't I deserve some respect?

Speaking of respect, what could garner more reverent acknowledgment than an obituary? Yet how many times do we see someone's death notice with absolutely no mention of their age? For goodness sake, these people are no longer here, and they still won't admit how old they are? I have a friend who said her mother would never reveal her age, and she certainly wouldn't want it published in the paper in her obituary.

To me that's taking the pretension of youth a little too far. I often read obituaries and am taken in by stories of people who have led full lives. I find some of their ages remarkable. There's nothing like dying of old age.

Well before an accounting of our lives appears in the paper, many of us still want to hide the fact that we've been on earth longer than other people. Why do we do this? Because we think the majority of people who haven't been around as long as we have will stop taking us seriously. ("How could they know anything? They're too old.")

Seriously? Think about what you're thinking: because we're older we know *less* about life than someone who hasn't been here as long? No, you're thinking, we're less hip because we've been here *too long*. We're out of the zeitgeist. And I know what you mean. Sometimes I think I have my fingers on the zeitgeist when most of the time the zeitgeist is slipping through them.

But is this important? It's like how you look when you're on the beach. When we were in our twenties we looked great on the beach because we were in our reproductive years, and human beings are supposed to look good in bathing suits when they're trying to attract mates. Today we're not trying to reproduce. Isn't that a good thing? We're simply trying to enjoy our lives and find peace and happiness in the process.

By the same token, young people are supposed to be up on what's going on in their age group because their social interactions, and maybe their livelihoods, depend on it. They are at a different stage in life. It's appropriate for them to have their own idea of what's cool. It's how they communicate their status to one other. But since we're at a more advanced stage of life, we don't have to go along with their ideas if they don't suit us.

If you decide it's okay not to be on the cusp of what younger people think is hip and you reveal your age, what will happen? For one thing, you will help dispel the idea that telling your age is taboo. You will remind them that oldness is not a fate worse than, well, you know.

When you tell people your age, you're saying it's perfectly fine to be fifty-eight or sixty-three or seventy-five. It's where you are in life. You've earned the right to be older because you've accumulated the years. Young people can't help it if they are not as advanced as you are.

I give myself context when people know I'm old enough to remember Dwight Eisenhower as president, that I was in high school when Kennedy was assassinated and was a young wife and pregnant when I watched men land on the moon. I've seen a lot. Ask me what America was like in the 1950s or during the Vietnam War or the Watergate hearings. See, you know quite a bit about me already.

If I'm pretending to be younger than I am, though, I'm not being true to my older, authentic self. I'd have to pretend I don't know any of that stuff.

Owning up to your age also helps remove the stigma of ageism and nudge our paradigm shift forward. If older people won't admit their age, they are sending the message that there's something wrong with being their age, and you've read enough of this book by now to know there's nothing wrong with being any age.

Reaching elderhood is the pinnacle of human achievement. It's where younger people want to end up. Why else would they continue to exercise, watch their weight, monitor their blood pressure, stop smoking? Why else, for heaven's sake, are they cutting down on bacon? Because they want to live longer. You've done what they want to do. Congratulations.

If you start to see yourself as an advanced human who can be a role model for younger people on their way to becoming advanced humans, your attitude about age might change. Think about this for a moment:

The pain wrinkles inflict is entirely of our own making.[1]

> William H. Thomas, MD
> *What Are Old People For?*

Part of the reason we don't want to admit our age has to do with the way we look. We may not want to bring attention to it. We have more wrinkles now than we used to. We may weigh more than we once did. Muscle tone may not be what it was. It's normal to feel a sense of loss over these physical changes. But rather than be curious about them (and think to ourselves, "So this is what it's like to age"), we battle against them.

Look, if you want to get wrinkle injections or even a facelift, if having a dermatologic procedure will help you feel better about yourself, then by all means do it. But remember, wrinkles are not some outgrowth of disease. They are not painful. They are the natural result of living awhile. If you intend to live longer, you will probably have more of them.

Seeing your older face and body in a new way, with a sense of discovery and even humor (maybe the way you saw your adolescent body as it was developing), can be a lot more soothing to your psyche than fighting the aging process. And it can be a lot less damaging to your bank account than plastic surgery. When you let yourself age naturally, you are letting go of the stress of having to be something you're not—young. You're revealing more of the real you.

When you offer the real you, you don't become prey to other people's immense neediness, or to their capacity to take advantage. Rather, you become stronger.[2]

> Deepak Chopra
> *Reinventing the Body,*
> *Resurrecting the Soul.*

Maybe we need new role models. Most of society's role models are young people—actors, rock stars, football players. Even older role models tend to be of the skydiving octogenarian nature. What about role models we can relate to? Role models who are okay with aging and aren't out to prove anything? Older people who reinforce our curiosity and enthusiasm about our aging selves and offer us ways to make the most of our own uniqueness?

There is a wonderful website called Advanced Style (www. advanced.style). Created by Ari Seth Cohen, it applauds older men and women who have developed their own unique approach to fashion. These are people who are not afraid to feel good about their age. They don't look like post-facelift patients who've bought into the idea that younger is better. They look like folks who are having the time of their lives.

> Maybe people who have facelifts should have a family reunion. Because they look so much alike.
>
> Kathleen O.

To me a good role model is someone engaged in "being," someone who smiles and has a kind, accessible face as if it would be easy to know him or her. Someone who is curious about life and other people, content with where she's been, and alive with interest in the future. Maybe someone who's a little eccentric and not afraid to be herself.

> Every time you speak your truth, you are advancing your own evolution.[3]
>
> Deepak Chopra
> *Reinventing the Body,*
> *Resurrecting the Soul.*

There is something ridiculously fun about being eccentric. There is something truthful about it too. It's as if the most interesting parts of you are peeking out from behind a screen of conformity. And there is no better time than later life to let your inner eccentric shine through. Have you always wanted to get a tattoo? Have you wanted to dress in lots of bright colors? Or put purple streaks in your hair? What's stopping you?

As he ages, Thomas Moore, former monk and psychotherapist, characterizes his liberation from convention this way:

> "I pursue my interest in UFOs and aliens, develop my skills with the scrying mirror [a device used to foretell the future] and use my intuition as the main guide of my life. I find personal strength in those eccentricities."[4]

It's worth noting that Moore uses the word *strength* when describing what he gains from being eccentric. When you come out from behind the curtain, you are reinforcing a confidence in yourself. You are being honest about who you are.

You are settling comfortably into your own skin. You can also serve as a role model for others who may want to express their own originality but aren't sure how to do it.

What aligns nicely with a display of eccentricity is data showing older people are a distinctly non-homogeneous group. Robert Butler points out in *The Longevity Revolution*, ". . .there is increasing variability among people as they grow older. . .Children are much more like one another than are 'the elderly.'"[5] As Dr. Louise Aronson, professor of geriatrics at the University of California, San Francisco, puts it: "When you've seen one eighty-year-old, you've seen one eighty-year-old,"[6] meaning each older person has a unique way to age. It is time to spread your wings and your eccentric tendencies around.

If you want to indulge in some eye-catching behavior, you could always wear a *chanchanko* (red coat) and a *zukin* (red cap) and sit on a *zabuton* (red cushion) on your sixtieth birthday. All are part of the ancient Japanese custom of wearing red on the day you turn sixty. Red symbolizes the beginning of the next cycle of your life, and in Japan, it's as if you become a baby again. You start over. (Babies in Japan are called *aka-chan* or "red one").

Though many Japanese no longer wear the traditional coat and cap, they often wear red on their sixtieth and celebrate with family and friends. You could say it's a "right" of passage. Perhaps a rite of passage is something that would help all of us transition a little more comfortably into elderhood. Other cultures fete people as they enter their later years, why don't we?

In Ivory Coast tribal culture, after a person has, as the Hindus would call it, lived as a Householder (adult) and has been part of the community, he or she is honored by induction into the Elder circle[7]. The Elders (usually sixty-five and older) are considered "masters of the school of life."[8] They are in charge of tribal rituals, they guard cultural secrets, and pass on their wisdom to younger members of the tribe through storytelling.

These Elders have an important role in their society because they *are* the older members of society. My guess is they're not preoccupied with erasing wrinkles or acting younger than their age.

What if we instituted our own rites of passage? We could help one another celebrate our entry into our later years, on a special birthday, for instance. In Denmark when people turn fifty or sixty they throw open their homes for a birthday "open house." They put an ad in the paper, and people come by over the course of the day to eat, drink, and mark the occasion of the person getting older. We may not want to put an ad in the paper (unless we want to make a lot of new friends), but we could certainly host a daylong open house to exult in our newfound role as a fifty, sixty, seventy, or eighty-year-old.

When my dad turned sixty-five, my mother had a "This is Your Life" party for him, modeled after the old 1950s TV program. His two brothers, people from his past who came from out of town, friends from in town, and immediate family were sequestered in my parents' basement as the surprise party got underway upstairs. One by one each guest came into the living room to tell funny and sweet stories about dad.

I had never seen him have so much fun. All those people from his past and present in his living room to mark an important day for him. He retired shortly after the party to enjoy a wonderful elderhood filled with traveling, reading, writing, and taking classes. The party acted as a rite of passage for him—a way to acknowledge his past, and as a marker to welcome his elderhood, which he enjoyed with a sense of liberation.

What all these rites of passage have in common, whether we call them rites or not, is that they help people feel more at home with growing older. When we honor rather than bemoan the time that has passed, we encourage ourselves to be grateful for what has gone before and look ahead to what will come. It's a way of nurturing our own life, whether we're looking back on it or moving forward into it.

When I was a young girl I used to cut out pictures of glamorous people from magazines and put them on a wall in my closet. They were usually movie or TV stars, models, or famous singers. I would look at the photos and wish I could be like those people, either look like they did, or have their abilities. They were role models for me.

Today I cut out pictures of older people in magazines, people who look especially appealing in some way. I cut out stories about intriguing, older people too. They are my role models now. They remind me how captivating older people can look and be.

Collecting clippings of my new role models is part of my rites of passage. They reinforce that I am in a different time in my life, an important time, with the maturity to handle what's coming with more mastery, not unlike the people featured in the saved articles.

In one newspaper photo I cut out, an older couple is dancing together. The woman, in a short, filmy dress, has turned her head to look directly at her partner with an appealing, slightly crooked smile, while the man is concentrating on his footwork. They don't look like a typical couple, maybe because they're enjoying themselves unselfconsciously. I want to be like they are. At this point in my life, it's ridiculous not to be.

❬**Pinpoint** *some of the ways you can*
feel better about the older you.❭

What do you like most about yourself? Your sense of humor? Your doggedness in solving a problem? Your long, graceful fingers? Write these things down and think of all the meaningful ways you've evolved over the decades— all the skills, the emotional maturity, and the perspective you've developed.

Would you ever want to be twenty again? How about a redo on thirty, forty, or even fifty? If not, why not?

How would you celebrate a rite of passage into elder-hood? What are some fun and meaningful ways to pro-claim your entry into this new stage of life?

Who are your role models now?

What can you learn from them, and how can they make you feel better about your aging self?

Now that you've dyed your hair pink, booked your birthday trip to Vegas, told everyone your age (unnerving a few people on the elevator), and plastered Iris Apfel all over your fridge, you're ready for your close-up. A close-up that will focus deep inside your pretty pink head to the very essence of you.

Chapter Eight
Know Thy Aging Self.

As Socrates put it, there is nothing like getting to know yourself as you grow older. Well, he might have said that if he'd been more enthusiastic about old age and less so about hemlock.

But Socrates's admonition to "know thyself" (as he apparently put it in Plato's dialogues) is advice that has been handed down for thousands of years. It was considered ancient wisdom in Socrates's time. A variation of "knowing thyself" is also a hallmark of Eastern religious thought.

"See your true nature, become Buddha."[1]

Zen Master Seung Sahn

Buddhism is about letting go of the ego to see your true nature. Going inward, whether to dissolve your ego or understand it better so you can dissolve it if you want to, is one of life's great journeys.

". . .our happiness, satisfaction, and our understanding. . . will be no deeper than our capacity to know ourselves inwardly. . ."[2]

Jon Kabat-Zinn *Wherever You Go There You Are*

From Carl Jung:

> "The privilege of a lifetime is to become who you truly are."[3]

And Deepak Chopra:

> "Go inside and meet yourself."[4]

Getting to know ourselves sounds like a good idea, but don't we know ourselves already?

We do and we don't. We probably know ourselves better now than we did when we were younger and still experimenting with our possible personas, the potential outward selves we could become. We probably know ourselves better than we did in middle age.

But truly knowing yourself involves reflection. With life swirling around you in your earlier years, it might not have been possible to examine you with the thoroughness you deserved.

So, are our later years the best years to go inward and find our true selves?

Well, they're the only years we have. We're kind of running out of time. But yes, to end this paragraph on a high note, the desire for exploring our true nature as we age is, apparently, biologically programmed.

If you'll recall, we talked about the concept of life review, dubbed by Robert Butler and noted in his book *Why Survive?*

Being Old in America. This is a process that appears to cut across cultural lines and goes on among those in later life. Life review takes place when older people look back on their lives and assess where they've been, and they contemplate who they are and what life has meant to them. According to Butler,

> "The old are not only taking stock of themselves as they review their lives, they are trying to think and feel through what they will do with the time that is left and with whatever emotional and material legacies they may have to give to others."[5]

In case you find this is a bit of a downer (particularly his reference to "time that is left"), Butler goes on to an upbeat finish.

> "Other researchers have found that increased and intense introspection . . . [leads] to a more serene and tranquil disposition."[6]

Maybe there's a point to life review after all. We have a built-in way to feel better about growing old and our later life. Nature's Xanax.

Butler also talks about "life review therapy" as a way to draw out older people and give them an opportunity to tell their stories to a therapist or loved one and to hear that story themselves, as they tell it.

Life review exercises have been incorporated into some elder workshops, teaching older people how to trace their lives from childhood to adulthood to present day. The purpose is to have participants look back on where they've been to better understand where they'd like to go.

You could say this is a kind of "forced" life review because it isn't the natural process Butler described, but perhaps it can affect our own natural process or even speed it up.

Anyway, it makes sense that knowing ourselves probably begins with reviewing where we've been.

> "'Man,' he says, drawing out the single syllable. 'It's cool to revisit how I got here.'"[7]
>
>> Jon Batiste, band leader of *The Late Show with Stephen Colbert*, as told to *Wall Street Journal Magazine*

It is cool. It's cool to think about how our childhood, adolescence, and adulthood have affected the way we live our lives now. If we want to change our lives, then reexamining those times may help.

I'm no psychologist, but I've been to one. They're always asking you about your childhood. Then they ask you how you feel about it. I figure we can save you a little money and cut to the chase.

Tell yourself about your childhood. Then ask yourself how you feel about it.

Here are a few "life review" questions to get you started, the kind you might come across if you took a class on constructing your own life analysis. This is as good a time as any to reflect on your past and learn more about what makes you you. Write down what first comes to mind.

1. What are my earliest memories? Why do I think these memories have stayed with me so long?

2. Picture myself as a child. How did I look? What did I like to do? How do I feel about these recollections? (Happy? Do I have mixed feelings? Melancholy? Sad? Why do I think I feel this way?)

3. Who was my best friend (friends) when I was growing up? Why was I attracted to him or her? Have I kept in touch with this person? How do I think this person would describe me as a child?

4. What one thing would I change about my childhood if I could? Is there more than one thing? Why would I change it? Did these events or circumstances affect my later life? Why not?

You can probably come up with more questions to ask yourself as you go inward. Some of the memories may be painful. You may or may not want to look at them in greater depth (or you may want to look at them with help from a professional). Whatever you decide to focus on is fine.

I'm not fond of thinking about the not-so-good times, not that there were that many of them.

But for our purposes here, we can certainly concentrate on what made us happy as children. Even when it comes to thinking about the changes we would've made to our child-hood. Because chances are the *kinds* of things that made us feel good then probably still appeal to us now. And we can incorporate more of our favorite indulgences into our current lives.

Did you like to read? Play outdoors? Spend time with friends? Spend quality time alone? Did you have imaginary play-mates? (Don't try this now.) But did you enjoy using your imagination? Did you like to write stories or draw or paint? Did you put on plays with friends? Take dance lessons? Play an instrument? Think about the games you played. Are there some similarities to games you enjoy now?

Taking note of these parts of yourself can remind you of what have always been your touchstones. Do the things you en-gage in now measure up to the activities or non-activities you were attracted to as a child?

It's important to write all of this down. The act of writing un-derscores the meaning these memories have for you.

"I want to write about me, my discoveries, my fears, my feelings, about me."

Helen Keller

Let's keep writing. Take the questions you answered above about your childhood and apply a similar survey to your adolescence.

1. What were your earliest memories of your teenage years?

2. What did you enjoy doing?

3. Who were your friends? Why did you like them?

4. What one thing would you change about your adolescence?

5. How was your adolescence different from your childhood?

Adolescent years were tough sledding for a lot of us. Many of my friends say they don't have particularly good memories of high school. It was a time when they began to see who they were. Sometimes the person they were didn't fit into the conformist thinking of all the people who were enthusiastically enjoying high school. Don't you wish you could go back and tell the adolescent you that everything is going to be okay?

Maybe you already have, by looking tenderly back at your young self and recording your thoughts. As therapist Ron Pevny put it in his online article, "The Inner Work of Conscious Eldering," "The awareness we gain [from a life review] is what makes virtually all the other inner work possible and effective."[8]

Pevny is talking about the inner work of gathering self-knowledge through all the life stages. But I also think knowing ourselves adds to our store of wisdom in general. To have a more intimate understanding of who you are, from childhood through old age, is to gain a deeper appreciation of everyone else. This is part of human maturity.

Learning about your own makeup includes reexamining your young adult and midlife years too. You've spent more time as an adult than in any other life stage. What can you gain from going back over these more recent years?

More questions to answer, you're thinking. And more work than I want to do, you're also thinking. I'm trying to read here.

Fair enough. But we can benefit from reexamining our adult years as an older person. We can see our adult selves more objectively now and learn from the things that gave us pleasure and fulfillment then, and also from what we didn't like so much.

If we enjoyed our work in our fifties but didn't like our boss, that's an easy fix. We can *be* something now that gives us the same good feelings as our work did without the bothersome boss. When we separate out the agreeable work from the person looking over our shoulder, we are coming to know ourselves in a new way.

Try this little adult-life review. You can keep it short by doing it in stages, maybe dividing it up into young adult, middle adult, and older adult, up to elderhood.

Let's look at your midlife years, for instance, taking in the big picture.

1. If you had to sum up your fifties in one or two sentences, what would you say?

2. What was your family like during this time? Describe your relationships with your children and your grandchildren. How about your spouse or partner? Your parents? Did you enjoy your connections with each of them?

3. Were there any significant family events that affected you in your fifties? How do you feel about these experiences now?

4. Did you take on any new caregiving roles? What impact did they have on you?

5. Were you working outside the home? Did you like your job? What did you like best about it? What did you like least?

6. What work accomplishments pleased you the most? (Not just the promotions, but maybe the way you handled a difficult situation.)

7. How was your overall health during this decade (mental and physical)? Did you have to come to terms with a medical condition? How did it affect you?

8. What was your most memorable vacation? Did it have a lasting impact on you? How important is travel to you?

9. Did you give much thought to your spiritual life in your fifties? Did you attend religious services? What spiritual changes did you experience?

10.If you could sum up midlife in one sentence, what would it be?

How do you feel about your life review so far? I know. You're tired of answering questions.

Remember the purpose of a life review is not to dredge up worn baggage but to find out more about who you are. By the way, if you've navigated through some tough times, those experiences are part of learning about you too.

In our later years it's important to concentrate on what is joyous about life, not what drags us down. It may be appropriate to put a little distance between you and some of the murky, unpleasant feelings from your past. In fact detaching from negativity is an essential part of Eastern thought, as the Dalai Lama explains:

> *"Actually the practice of Dharma is a constant battle within, replacing previous negative conditioning or habituation with new positive conditioning."*[9]

> [Dharma cannot be perfectly translated into English, but it generally refers to the teachings of the Buddha.]

As the Dalai Lama puts it:

> *"The turning-toward happiness as a valid goal and the . . . decision to seek happiness. . .can profoundly change the rest of our lives."*[10]

Knowing what makes us happy and following our heart's longings can open a new passage for us as we age. Going inside ourselves and finding contentment there is in itself a "valid goal" of aging.

We aren't the only ones who can help sort out our essence. Those dear to us can often bring to light aspects of ourselves we may have missed. It is enormously comforting to hear good words from others.

There is a psychology model called the Johari Window, created by Joseph Luft and Harry Ingham in 1955.[11] It's used as a technique to better understand our relationship with ourselves and those around us. A friend of mine who is a clinical psychologist drew the diagram for me on a napkin one afternoon when we were having lunch.

As you can see, the Window is a square divided into four parts. It shows us that knowing ourselves also incorporates insight from other people. The most obvious information you have about yourself is in the far left, upper quadrant: What you know about you, and what others know about you.

The neighboring quadrant to the right includes a way to see yourself that perhaps you hadn't thought of: What others know about you, but you don't know about yourself.

The bottom left section is kind of the flip side of this: What you know about yourself that others don't.

Then finally, what you don't know about yourself, and others don't know about you either.

This exercise is provocative. There are parts of you you're unaware of, and other people can fill in the blanks, but there are sides to you that no one knows about. How can that be? Apparently, humans are complicated.

When my friend first described the Johari Window to me, I was fascinated, especially with the right, top quadrant. What do people know about me that I don't know?

It might be illuminating to have this Johari section revealed to you.

There may be parts of you that, once uncovered, could transform the way you see yourself. For the better. But I would suggest going to someone you trust and you know cares about you. Ask *her* what she knows about you that you don't know. Don't ask your misanthropic brother-in-law. You want to luxuriate in this newfound knowledge.

Let's think for a moment how we can take what we are learning about us and translate our emerging awareness into a happier elder life. Certainly when we are more familiar with who we are, we can be more in touch with how we feel day to day. And we can learn to take care of ourselves in more loving ways.

Tenzin Wangyal Rinpoche, a Bon teacher, (Bon being the ancient, Tibetan shaman tradition), has advice for us:

> If we are "in a rush and feel agitated". . .we may want to "embrace stillness and let the illusion of time wash over us." "If we are speaking negatively to ourselves or others", we may want to "practice silence".

> "If. . . life's stresses are feeling too close or heavy, Tenzin Wangyal Rinpoche "asks that we give ourselves some mental and emotional space from these external or imagined stimuli."[12]

In other words, like Paul Salopek's "A Stroll Around the World" in chapter six, Tenzin is asking us to change our perspective. This time he's talking about going inward to see the world differently.

How do we do this? How do we separate ourselves from our disquiet and concentrate on the happiness we're trying to encourage?

It has to do with staying in the moment, when possible. Putting aside unwanted thoughts, and being, at this very instant, present with what is going on with you.

Ram Dass calls it ". . . mak[ing] a conscious effort to live with 'beginner's mind,' coming to each experience fresh. . ."[13]

> *Prolong not the past*
> *Invite not the future*
>   *. . .There is nothing more than that.*[14]
>
>   Tibetan Buddhist saying

One way to train ourselves to do this, to live in a new "present moment" way, is through meditation. It is a tool that can help us zero in on what is happening at this point in time and go deep within ourselves. The act of meditating can even cause us to feel as if there is no time. Only the now. Which is a very Eastern inclination.

Unless you're a Buddhist monk (and if you are, I should be reading *your* book), you may not be able to sustain a lifetime of living only in the present. But the more you let go of unwanted thoughts from the past and worry less about what will happen in the future, the more you will live in the present. It's a luminous spot to settle into.

Buddhist monks (who could be called habitual meditators) participated in a neuroscience research project through the University of Wisconsin in 2002. Cognitive scientist Dr. Richard Davidson found that the monks produced "thirty times more gamma waves" (signaling intense thought) than the control group of non-meditating students. And "much larger areas of [the monks' brains] were activated during compassion meditation, especially in the left prefrontal cortex."[15] That's the area where our positive emotions reside.

If you're not a monk but you meditate anyway, you're also going to get a mood boost, more focus in your daily activities, stress reduction, and maybe even a stronger immune system. This comes from other studies of meditators, including high-tech workers trained in mindfulness meditation.[16]

Aren't we always reading that meditating can have emotional, intellectual and health benefits?

So how does this meditation thing work? Do you have to do it every day? And what if you've tried it a few times, but you can't seem to get the hang of it?

First of all, you don't have to do it. At this age, you don't have to do anything you don't want to do. But Jon Kabat-Zinn has some good advice for those of us who feel meditating is going to be a difficult or time-consuming practice.

> "There is nothing magical or mystical about meditation. Basically, it is about paying attention, purposely, in the only time you have to live, namely this present moment."[17]

There it is again: it's about the moment. *Being* in the moment. Not *trying* to do something. Focusing on the wonderful state of what is present. What is right now.

It's like learning to ride a bike or learning to swim. All of a sudden you're pedaling down the block on your new two-wheeler, and Dad isn't holding on. You look back, and there he is on the sidewalk, several houses away. You're riding. You're not *trying* to ride. You are *being* a rider on a bike. It's easy.

Or you're in the pool and Mom is holding you up as you kick and move your arms, and then you find you're kicking and moving your arms, and Mom has let go. You swim to the edge of the pool all by yourself. Right at that moment you are *being* a swimmer. It seems natural.

Meditating is like that. It's not hard when you stop trying and simply let go.

To meditate is to do something secular. The act itself can be embraced by the devoutly faithful who may use it as part of their religious observance. Or atheists can do it. There are different kinds of meditation: transcendental, mindfulness, compassionate, Buddhist, Hindu, Jewish, Christian, Sufi. Almost every major religion has a meditation practice. And some people just enjoy meditating to their own special drummer.

I first learned to meditate through a course on mindfulness meditation. It's a method that stresses calmness but also awareness. You don't ignore thoughts that arise while you're meditating, but you make note of them, without judging them, as they float through your mind.

Transcendental meditation is similar, but instead of observing stray thoughts during meditation, you gently push them aside and come back to a focus on breathing or a mantra (a sound or words you repeat over and over).

I like to combine both types of meditation. Sometimes I try to look at thoughts that come into my mind with objective interest, but I also find that if I get caught up in looking at my thoughts, I can lose that feeling of relaxation and the peace I find going inward. I tend to concentrate (or not concentrate, as enthusiasts would say) on a visual that produces a mellowing effect.

I visualize an ocean beach, a mountain pasture, a garden in the sunlight, a farm field stretching out around me. These can be places I've been, pictures I've seen or even surroundings I only imagine. Focusing on breathing is important too. It helps you center yourself and be present to what is happening when you take air in and then exhale it.

Before we begin to meditate, it may be helpful to note the words of Giovanni Dienstmann from his website Live and Dare:

> "Our brain is. . .wired to. . . seek pleasure. So, if you can generate some stable feelings of safety and contentment, right before your meditation, you are sending a message to your brain that all is well, and it need not be restless."[18]

Let's *try* this. Keeping the concept of "effort" at bay, if you can. Let's do another meditation exercise like the ones I've already sprinkled in the book.

First of all, find a quiet place. You can meditate anywhere, but when you are starting out, it's good to be in a place where the surroundings are already calm.

Take a deep breath. Blow it out slowly. Take another breath. Breathe in slowly and then exhale again. Envision the air going gently and deeply into your lungs and belly. How satisfying it is to know that this essential thing, breathing, is for most of us effortless.

Close your eyes. Stop visual stimuli from coming into your brain. If it's quiet and you're not looking at anything, it will be easier to focus on your breath.

Now visualize a beautiful setting, maybe a place you've visited, a photo you've seen, a location that brings back happy feelings.

Or envision a word. Like peace, stillness, harmony, happiness. Say the word to yourself over and over. The repetition will help you concentrate.

If thoughts or sounds seep in, you can observe them nonjudgmentally. Turn them over and around to see they are merely thoughts, then let them go. Or you can gently move the intrusion aside. Come back to your special vision or your mantra (the word or words you've chosen).

If you'd like to have music in the background, pick something that won't distract you. You don't want to be humming along.

Always return to your breath. You are alive. Sometimes we forget to pay attention to that.

You can meditate anywhere. There is a thing called "walking meditation" where you can be immersed in your breathing while you wander through a park. You can meditate every day, or once a week, if that's what you want to do. The more you go into the intimate state of awareness with yourself, the greater your own appreciation of all your moments will be.

I am not an expert on meditation.

Wait. You're not?

No, but I don't think you have to be one to enjoy the practice. You don't have to do it "right." You just have to do it. Or should we say, *be* it. Be one who meditates.

The idea of becoming familiar with you, knowing who you are, is not some useless abstraction. It has potency and substantive implications.

Yesterday I went to the art museum alone. I walked through an exhibit of works by Andrew Wyeth and his son, Jamie. I love the atmosphere in a museum—soft sounds, a respectful audience, walking from one painting to the next. As I looked at each piece of art and listened to the audio accompaniment, I found myself lost in the present. I was thoroughly experiencing what was before me with no thought of time or what I was going to fix for dinner.

I was in Pennsylvania with Andrew Wyeth, in Maine with Andrew and Jamie, looking out at glimpses of the sea through renderings of seagulls, clapboard houses, and the night sky. Did you know Jamie used a string of his wife's pearls, crushed, to make images of stars on the midnight canvas?

Andrew poured black ink on one of his almost-finished portraits, turned the painting upside down, and the rivulets of black running down the canvas became winter trees in the background.

This kind of creativity is inspiring. Anyone can be inspired by it. It reminds me to view the world with "beginner's mind." It means that, like the Wyeths, I too can be open to experimenting. I have always liked the idea of seeing life from an unorthodox perspective. Encouraging an openness that is already a part of me can make me a better writer. A better cook. Or even a better arranger of flowers for my dining room table.

> "As we live, we *learn* who we are, and
> with *self-knowledge* comes *self-belief*."[19]
>
>   Isabel Allende

The more you know about yourself, the more you will reinforce the essence of you, which is why being present is so important. You don't want to miss the little signals that cause the synapses of knowing to fire in your brain: These are my moments. This is part of what makes me who I am.

And who I am not.

The profound act of reflection can also help us weed out what keeps us from feeling happy. At this point in our lives, there may be things we don't want to do anymore. It's good to recognize them. Because another reason being old is so much fun is that we don't have to do what we really don't want to. With maybe two little exceptions.

CHAPTER NINE
You Don't Have to Do That Anymore.

There are exceptions. You do have to continue to pay taxes, though maybe not to the extent you used to. And you will pass on. To be precise, "die" is the word. But don't think about those things right now.

Think about the stuff you really don't want to do.

Here's what I don't want to do:

1. **Drive on a freeway at night**. I don't see as well as I used to. It's something about depth perception and bright lights. Schedule your jewelry party or cookie exchange during the day. Scratch that. I'm not going to another cookie exchange. Whatever you're having, I'm not coming if it's dark and you don't live a stone's throw away.

2. **Go to my friend's grandkid's soccer game**. Yes, your grandkids are adorable, but I don't want to spend the afternoon adoring them. I put in my time when my son played Little League. From now on you'll have to attend wildly entertaining events like these on your own.

3. **Fix Thanksgiving dinner**. I realize Thanksgiving is sacrosanct, and I like turkey as much as anyone. But I've

been cooking T-day dinner for fifty years now. Like the turkey never seems to be, I am done.

I want to glide into the festivities next year like everyone else. I want to sit down, hold a glass of wine in my hand, and chat with assorted guests. I told my son the next Thanksgiving feast is his to create. You know what? He said okay.

4. Have lunch with someone who drags me down. I have a nice number of friends, not too many. I like them all, but every once in a while a person enters my life who ends up being a lot of work. He or she is needy, negative. I feel bad about them. But I can't save them. So I try to pass on spending time with them.

I once read in an advice column that when negative people keep hounding you to get together, you should just tell those people you are "crazy busy," and you'll get back to them when the smoke clears. Of course it never does. Over time you'll end up distancing yourself from them—the self-absorbed—and they'll stop calling. You continue to have lunch with people whose friendships you value, and your indigestion goes away.

5. Schlep casseroles. If you're going to have a dinner party, either fix the meal yourself or pick up prepared food from the grocery. We're coming to enjoy you and the company of your sparkling guests. I do not want to "bring something." I am too old to travel through the city balancing food on my lap, only to have to take the leftovers back across town once the evening is over.

Doesn't it feel good to get that off my chest? I may sound curmudgeonly, but I think part of taking care of me is to parcel out my time in a way that will make me happy.

Not doing things you don't want to do is a matter of being honest with yourself. It's a way to ensure you are devoting these significant years to things you're keen on.

Let Cicero do the talking:

> *"Old age will only be respected when it fights for itself, maintains its rights, avoids dependence on anyone, and asserts control over its own to the last breath."*

While I may not agree with our Roman sage about dependence (sometimes we have to depend on others), I think he's right on about "fighting for ourselves." It seems we never have to fight as hard against people's expectations as we do when we get older.

We're supposed to stay young; we're supposed to disparage our own old age. We're charged with being good old people and putting others' needs ahead of our own. We're admired if we try to keep up with the younger set. I say phooey.

While I'm on a roll, here is a short list of things I'm refusing to try now that I'm older:

Skiing	I don't want to break anything, sprain anything, even bruise anything.

Surfing	See above.
Rock climbing	I have to explain this?
Wearing 5-inch heels	Ditto

Things I will try now that I'm older:

Fly fishing	It looks like it could be fun, though I'd feel sorry for the fish.
Snowshoeing	Tame enough for me. Plus it's good exercise.
Ziplining	This will come as a shock to my husband, but I wouldn't mind sliding along the tops of trees. As long as the trees aren't up too high.
Traveling to India	I have long been attracted to exotic places, and nothing to me is as intriguing as India.

Just trust yourself,
then you will know how to live.

Goethe

You've earned the right to say yes to some things and no to others. And you're old enough to know which is which. That nagging image of what old people are supposed to be needs to be shown the door.

Speaking of which, there is a humorous (well, it's humorous now) "self-help manual" that was published in 1829 by Reverend John Sanford called *The Aged Christian's Companion*.[1] Certainly the reverend didn't intend for anyone to find his book "adapted especially for those. . . entering the vale of years"[2] funny. But if you read about the path he proposes for older people, you'll realize we've come a long way.

A little excerpt:

> *"Aged men [should] be sober, grave, temperate, sound in faith, in charity, in patience.*
>
> *"[Old] women. . . [should] be in behavior that becomes holiness, [they should be] not false accusers, not given to much wine, teachers of good things. . ."[3]*

You lost me at wine. I suppose a few of these recommendations could be folded into our modern aging template. But the characteristics we want to adopt, or don't want to adopt, can be personal. Even if it has to do with faith, charity, and patience. Only you can sort out how you want to live the years ahead. That's part of the process of reclaiming your right to grow old.

Mihaly Csikszentmihalyi in his book *Flow* has some

illuminating guidelines for deciding how we might want to spend our time or not. *Flow*, as we've described, is all about getting into the moment, getting to a place where time almost stands still, where we are involved in something so fantastic that we can barely wrest ourselves from it.

How do we sort out undertakings that will bring on *flow* from those that won't? According to Csikszentmihalyi, the answer is centered in a gray area somewhere between anxiety and boredom. It boils down to this: we tend to experience *flow* when challenges and skills match up.

Let's say you are a painter. You like to draw and paint outdoor scenes, and it's easy for you to get into what Csikszentmihalyi calls the "*Flow* Channel"[4] when you're painting away. But you're getting a little tired of painting the same things, so you decide to attempt portrait painting. You've never tried it before. You start drawing portrait sketches, but you get frustrated. You're not sure your proportions are right. You become a bit unsure of your skills with the new subjects. You find you're not getting into the *flow*.

Before, you were bumping up against the zone of boredom. Now you're veering into anxiety territory.

Csikszentmihalyi would say you either need to ramp up your skills (take a class on portrait painting) or mitigate your challenges (maybe start with very simple pencil portraits). That's how you get back into that glorious *flow* space.

I think there's a third option. If you decide portrait painting is more than you bargained for, why not paint images you find less intimidating? Maybe not the landscapes that are becoming humdrum, but something other than portraits. How about a still life? You're the one who needs to be satisfied.

Somehow we get the idea that if we back down from a challenge, give up on it entirely, we succumb to a kind of indolence. We're just drifting along, not seeing things through. What a Western view that is.

When we're older and have a more complete sense of what we want to accomplish and what it takes to get there, we should be able to edit things out of our lives. That may include painting people who sit in wing chairs.

> "To let go means to give up coercing, resisting, or struggling, in exchange for something more powerful. . . It's akin to letting your palm open to unhand something you have been holding on to."[5]
>
> Jon Kabat-Zinn

What have you been holding onto? Maybe it's a house that's too large. Or an image of yourself as someone who's always available. How about a closet full of clothes you don't wear anymore? Some you don't even like. Why are you keeping them? Because they were an investment, and for some reason you feel obligated to store them forever? You're tired of your book club, but you think the people in it will be unhappy if you quit? What if you quit?

What could be more powerful than your own approval of how you're living day to day? What could be more exhilarating than unloading something you want gone from your life? When you let go of the things that no longer serve you, you make room for more of the things that do.

That in itself may be enough to kick-start another tantalizing round of *flow* in your routine.

And if there are days you feel like being lazy? The important thing is that you're *being*. Who cares if you're lazy? If you were thirty years younger, lots of people might care, but your desire to do nothing is part of the privilege of age. The concept of "have to" has to be eliminated.

What does it mean to do nothing? To have extended time without busyness? To be idle? It sounds heretical to Western ears, but an ancient Eastern take on a state of nothingness might be something quite different.

> *Stop talking, stop thinking,*
> *and there is nothing you will not understand.*[6]

>   Seng-Ts'an

Doing nothing may give us room to see our greater selves, a longing we may feel more pointedly as we get older. Just lying under an umbrella on a beach somewhere may be exactly the non-activity we need to get closer to our true essence.

And what is that? Ask the elder Hindu who is searching for

his spiritual self in his third stage of life. He is spending his days in restful contentment, unraveling the answer.

❮**Note** *some roles or duties you'd like to shed.*❯

What is it you don't want to do anymore? You've earned a pass on having to please everyone else. Now please *your-self* by crossing some things off your list.

CHAPTER TEN
Your Own Special Spiritual Quest.

Age is opportunity no less
Than youth itself, though in another dress,
And as the evening twilight fades away
The sky is filled with stars invisible by day.[1]

Longfellow

As we grow older there is something in the ether of our thoughts that is worth exploring. What is it? What is it that encourages us to dwell a bit more in an inner world that can open up to a world beyond us?

Do we become more spiritual as we age?

In 1380 Thomas Brinton, bishop of Rochester (England), preached that as we grow older, spiritual age progresses from "good to better, from perfection to greater perfection."[2] He felt aging and spiritual growth, or "ascent," went hand in hand.

On the downside, medieval Europeans burned witches at the stake (often older women) for probing too deeply into their aging, spiritual selves. In Asia Minor, on the other hand, spiritual elders held great influence over young monks and other religious followers in the earliest monasteries. Younger monks didn't see anything heretical in the reflections of their elders. In fact they copied their way of life and sought out their heaven-inspired advice.

Apparently Hindus think we become more spiritual as we grow older, or they wouldn't have allowed elders and their spiritual growth to take up two of their four life stages.

The actual beginning of elderhood, according to Hindu philosophy, is the third phase of life called "The Forest Retirement Stage." You don't literally retire to a forest, but as an older person, you're supposed to start thinking about what makes you tick. That's when you ask the big question: Who am I? The idea is to make time to "read, think, and consider the significance of life without the interruption of duty."[3] "No duties" sounds like grandpa can just snooze on the sofa. He can, as long as he's dreaming about his spiritual self.

The fourth stage in the Hindu life cycle is called "The Forest Dweller" or "Ascetic" period, and yes, you are supposed to move to the forest to contemplate detachment, death, and the reincarnation that is coming[4]. Of course *you* don't have to go to a forest. You can lie on a beach and think about this stuff. The point is, you no longer have to be "busy" if you don't want to be. You don't have any obligations, so you can focus on your inner journey.

If you're not a Hindu you can still borrow some of the ideas from Hindu thought and make them your own. With or without the rigor of religion, you can set out on a spiritual search and follow the path of other elders around the world.

Data show a large majority of older Americans believe "having a rich spiritual life contributes meaning to life." Baby boomers, in the same study, said that when they think about growing older, having a "rich spiritual life will be very important,"[5]

Is this something we should be engaged in? Is it time to begin our own spiritual adventure?

I think many of us are already on a spiritual adventure. The concept of the innate process we call life review means aging humans have a tendency toward exploring the transcendent. Contemplating our lives is an exercise of turning inward, after all. One could then argue the act of going inward is a spiritual one.

Reviewing our lives causes us, in part, to think about how we fit into the larger scheme of things. When we look at ourselves, past and present, we are forced to look at what we value and why. These are beliefs that are rooted in our marrow. Why do we think the way we do? This question involves how we view the world. In turn, we have to decide what the world is. Is it just what we see, or is there more to it?

Lars Tornstam has some thoughts. A Swedish academic, he is the driving force behind a theory called *geotranscendence*. His research indicates that as we age, there is inherently "a transcendent movement away from the materialistic . . . point of view common in the first half of life."[6] We become less interested in acquiring things. We also develop less rigidity about right and wrong. Time and space seem to have "blurred boundaries," and there is a "renewed interest in nature."

Torstams's research also suggests "The fear of death recedes," and this "shift [in attitude] is accompanied by an increase in life satisfaction."[7] Are these spiritual stirrings?

If we follow Tornstam's reasoning, it seems that shaping our vision of ourselves, the world around us, and even the universe may be work that finds its spark in old age.

Former fashion illustrator Polly Francis wrote in her nineties:

> "More than at any other time in my life, I seem to be aware of the beauties of our spinning planet and the sky above. . .I feel that old age sharpens our awareness."[8]

And here's what could be a startling conclusion to Tornstam's thesis from William Thomas: The reason younger and middle-aged people struggle achieving the same level of transcendence older people do may be that they're not ready for it. Their brains are simply immature,[9] as opposed to older people's brains that *are* mature and able to connect to the intangible in ways not available to everyone.

It sounds like we're more or less obligated to explore our spiritual selves because nature has given us the ability to follow through on this quest. We certainly can't waste a lifetime of experience, to say nothing of our highly developed minds .

Yet you may be feeling a tinge of reticence. You're thinking,

I'm not a monk. A spiritual quest sounds like a big commitment. What if I just want to play golf?

Then play golf, by all means. Some say teeing off in the early morning when the grass is wet with a glaze of dew is a spiritual experience. You're not obliged to devote all your time to rooting around in your transcendent side. Just being aware that that side exists can expand your appreciation of what it means to be in the world.

A spiritual journey can be a slow and beautifully meandering process. You don't have to be on it every day. As Polly Francis pointed out, by simply aging we may be more aware of the import and meaning of ordinary things. When we're on a golf course, taking in the grass and trees and even the bunkers, we can appreciate the beauty of the day. We can be present in the moments that make up our morning and open to the feel of the sun and air.

This awareness can have meaningful implications.

Ram Dass agrees.

> ". . .the willingness to open our eyes to the possibility of our larger Self can transform our aging process into a spiritual opportunity."[10]

What is a spiritual opportunity? It doesn't have to have a narrow interpretation. It may be there in the serenity of an early-morning round of golf.

I have a good friend who is an atheist. She was raised as a Catholic, fell away from the church, and never went back to religion. Can she be a spiritual person, then? I think she is.

She lives in the heart of a big city, and when she's out for a walk, she has been known to pick up stray bits of litter off the street and carry discarded cans or wrappers to a city trash bin. She takes heart in her connection to others downtown, and it is very much her "larger" self, I believe, who wants to help her neighborhood thrive. She wouldn't hesitate to give a lost tourist directions to the light rail or help an older gentleman carry a heavy grocery bag to his car. She's seventy-four, and as she has aged, she has felt an increasing responsibility to those around her.

She also loves to travel by herself and spend moments in places far from home, just absorbing her surroundings.

> "Sitting and gazing at things without a thought in your head is a very good form of prayer."[11]

> Gerald W. Hughes, S.J.

Nothing refreshes my friend more, she says, than a little hike in the mountains. I call her connections to others, nature, and places faraway spiritual.

I know another atheist, a retired Presbyterian minister, whose spiritual quest led him from belief to skepticism to non-belief. He spent much time going deep within himself to reckon with growing doubts about God and religion. He came to his own conclusion after years of contemplation and ministering to others.

An interesting aside, this man teaches classes in spirituality. He clearly believes you can be spiritual and an atheist. Perhaps he sees himself more like a Buddhist who believes in spiritual awakening but not in the traditional worshipping of God. Or maybe he's simply a spiritual atheist, comfortable with his own incongruity.

Yet, my friend's quest may not be over. Learning about ourselves and becoming intimate with our own beliefs is ongoing. Will he still feel the same about his atheism in the years to come?

A spiritual journey doesn't take a prescribed tract. Everyone's search is different. How do we do it then? How do we go on a spiritual quest? With great awareness.

A journey into your higher self involves recognizing who you are and how you feel about your place in the universe. You do it by being this older person you've become. By entering into elderhood and detaching yourself from middle-aged "doing." When you are "being" in the moment and are aware of what you're experiencing, you become open to spiritual exploration.

My ninety-four-year-old mother-in-law, Dorothy, didn't really intend to go on a spiritual quest. But in her late sixties she found herself on one.

She was a lifelong Episcopalian and enjoyed attending church on Sunday. One Sunday she was sitting in a pew, listening to the priest retell the story of Noah's Ark, and it struck her. Noah's Ark had nothing to do with the life she was living. The story didn't speak to her anymore. She wanted spirituality in her life, but she realized she wasn't getting it from her church.

She began to look around at other religious paths. She ended up joining a small Science of Mind (not to be confused with Scientology) church in her neighborhood. Twenty-five years later, though not mobile enough to attend church on Sundays, Dorothy reads excerpts from her monthly *Science of Mind* magazine every morning with a cup of hazelnut coffee. She prays, meditates, and is at peace with the philosophy she has found.

Mary Alice, seventy-three, born a Catholic, found Tibetan Buddhism ten years ago and attends her *tsonga* (congregation) on Sundays.

Barbara, sixty-eight, brought up as a Conservative Jew, now practices meditation and finds spirituality in her work as a certified healing touch practitioner.

Michael, fifty-nine, son of an Orthodox rabbi, no longer goes to services, except maybe on High Holy days. He meditates and takes Kabbalah (Jewish mysticism) classes.

Jim, an agnostic, finds his spiritual peace at age sixty-five on hiking trails in the woods.

Wendy, seventy-six, is a lifelong Catholic. She considers herself spiritual and even wrote her doctoral dissertation in psychology on how religion can affect a patient's psychotherapy. Her journey has kept her in the church, though through the years she has developed her own relationship with Catholicism and its teachings. If you ask her, she will tell you she is much more aware of her feelings about her faith now and where she parts ways with Catholic philosophy.

> Buddhist scripture says the Buddha, soon after his enlightenment, met a traveler on the road who was dazzled "by the Buddha's extraordinary radiance and peaceful presence." The man asked the Buddha, are you a god? The Buddha replied, no. The man then said, are you a wizard? The Buddha said, no. The traveler asked, are you a man? No, said the Buddha. Then what are you?

> The Buddha replied, "I am awake."[12]

Buddha means "one who is awake."[13] While most of us will not become buddhas in our lifetimes, our spiritual journeys can give us insight into the meaning of our existence, plus a sense of peace we might not have had when we were younger. If we develop awareness.

Dorothy, Mary Alice, Barbara, Michael, Jim, Wendy, my friend who is an atheist, and the former minister who is also one, would not be where they are spiritually if they hadn't explored their own belief systems and been aware of the moments where their spiritual needs were not being met. And hadn't also been mindful of moments where their transcendent selves flowered.

According to the sampling above, it appears you don't have to be religious to be spiritual. There is a difference. Timber Hawkeye, writing for the *Science of Mind* journal (I got it from my mother-in-law!) says this:

> "I believe religion asks us to believe in someone else's experience, while spirituality invites us to have our own."[14]

Dr. David Sanders, executive director of Kabbalah Experience in Denver, seems to agree:

> When you take up a religion, you're taking up an "obligation" to be part of that religion. You follow the parameters of your faith to seek the divine. Spirituality, on the other hand, is more a free-will search for "God." You determine your own parameters.

Do you have to believe in God to be a spiritual seeker? Atheists and agnostics who have a spiritual side don't think so. Mary Alice, the Tibetan Buddhist, doesn't think so. Dorothy perceives "God" now in a different way, and so does Michael. These people have found a free-form way of looking at religion, transcendence and their place in the grand scheme, as David Sanders suggests.

If you follow a religious tradition and you're happy with it, as Wendy is, maybe your spiritual search means burrowing more deeply into the sacred beauty that attracts you to your religion. You can read religious texts, travel to holy sites with your congregation, or join a faith study group.

Thomas Moore, author of *A Religion of One's Own*, offers this: "To foster your spiritual life, you need an effective method especially suited to you."[15] I think he's right, and "especially suited to you" are key words. Though Moore does go on to say in his book that you need to be a "mystic" of sorts too.

"This is not an option," he says. "To be fully human you need some sort of mystical experiences regularly. Nature and art become especially important. . ."[16] as platforms for spiritual serendipity.

My guess is he's not talking about crazy, out-of-body occurrences. He is describing the art of being in the moment with a recognition of truth as you know it, and transcendence.

Even Csikszentmihalyi has an opinion on mysticism: *"Flow and religion have been connected from earliest times. Many of the optimal experiences of mankind have taken place in the context of religious rituals."*[17]

Or in the context of hiking in the woods, as Moore might add.

I have had my mystical experiences too, more along the line of what Moore alludes to.

I stood on Independence Pass, twelve thousand feet up in the Rocky Mountains and felt timelessness surrounding me. The landscape is so quiet you can hear the wind. There is something about the Pass that is both harsh and enfolding. I felt a connection to its barrenness and openness the first time I stood along the side of the road, above the timberline.

I've been here before, I thought. I belong here. I wanted to lie down on the tundra and look up at the dark blue sky. I wanted to be here at night to see the stars and planets sparkling above. I wanted to live here forever.

I have been to Independence Pass several times, for brief stops. I always feel the same mystical bond with its delicate ecosystem. There are signs that tell you not to walk on the dirt and scrubby plants that make up the tundra. It's a fragile place, though it can be formidable. The same could be said for much of creation, including us.

My spiritual story has been a journey from Protestant upbringing to agnosticism, to a belief in a greater power (perhaps *essence* is a better word) and the oneness of things. I've borrowed from many religions to erect a spiritual framework that satisfies me both intellectually and philosophically. I am still learning.

Every church has a membership of one.[18]

Emerson

Ultimately each of us has a personal way of viewing the cosmos and our part in it. I feel most transcendent when I am in a moment of timelessness and I perceive what is around me as both ancient and new. I like what Eckhart Tolle says about time in *A New Earth*: The elimination of time . . . is the only true spiritual practice.[19]

To me it's about being in that momentary space where we are in the absolute present and we're aware that we are. We may have an inkling that maybe this is all there is, one ephemeral moment in a universe that is endless. The words I used to say in church make more sense to me as an older person: as it was in the beginning, is now, and ever shall be, world without end. Amen.

It does seem the older we are, our practiced brains are able to see meaning in things that used to pass right by us when we were young. This is why a spiritual journey is so well suited to our older selves. We have the maturity and we have the time. Innately we probably have the will.

If you decide to take up your own spiritual pursuit, you might want to begin by seeing where you've been, spiritually. Here are a few questions to think about:

How did I feel about religion as a young person? Was my family religious, somewhat religious, agnostic, atheist?

Did I enjoy attending religious services as a child? If so, why? If not, why not?

(I have a friend, raised as an Orthodox Jew who used to feign sickness when the Sabbath rolled around and his parents wanted him to attend services. As a child he was bored with the long rituals. But as an adult he is an observant Jew, though not intent on following every obligation of his orthodox upbringing.)

Have my views on religion and spirituality changed? When did my feelings about faith begin to shift?

How do I feel about religion and spirituality in general?

Have I ever had a mystical experience? How would I describe this/these moments?

Do I think it's possible to be spiritual and not practice a religion or believe in God?

What would I like to get out of a spiritual journey?

Am I looking for a community of others on a similar path?

What kind of awareness do I need to be open to spiritual experiences?

You can enhance your journey by being mindful of and curious about the spiritual possibilities around you. They're almost everywhere. In nature, in art, in music, in a conversation, on a walk, at a religious service. You can also meditate, find a group with similar views to yours, or read up on other religions and spiritual practices, even if you're not sure you're open to them at this point. Go online and find blogs with spiritual themes. There is always something to take away from the contemplations of others.

Keep a spiritual journal. Okay, some people may not be over-joyed with this suggestion. It's too time-consuming, you're thinking, or you're so over the idea of journaling. But diary-keeping goes back to tenth-century Japan, and it is a wonder-ful Eastern (and Western) way to track your impressions. Find a notebook with an interesting cover and write down a few thoughts.

I've been keeping my own spiritual journal for a while, and it includes everything from reactions to *Shir Hadash* (Sing for Joy/ Sing for Renewal) Passover services I attended at a Conservative synagogue to a visit to my hometown church for communion to sitting on a cushion at a Buddhist *tsonga* on a Sunday morning. I don't write long entries. But I do make note of how I interpret these experiences. They have an impact on me.

> "Feel that you have a right to learn from and practice any-thing from the world's spiritual and religious traditions. They are yours. . .embrace the traditions or explore your agnosticism."[20]
>
> Thomas Moore, *A Religion of One's Own*

These words are empowering. Yes, adopt, borrow, explore, join a congregation, or just visit one. See what's out there. A spiritual quest should be fun, a little like a buffet. Sample what appeals to you. Then bring home your reflections to your journal or consider gathering little treasures from your experiences.

I have a number of icon-like objects on my desk that I've collected throughout my spiritual undertakings. They reflect religious traditions that have meaning for me. I like looking at them when I'm working. They transmit a peacefulness and a bit of the eternal that I find comforting when I'm frazzled. I dust them, rearrange them, add to them. You can do something similar at your desk or by your bedside or in your closet, as one of my friends does. She calls it her sacred space.

Part of learning to love your aging self is to find ways to bring comfort into your life and put a caring focus on you.

Your own, special spiritual trip can be wondrous, and it can engender calm and reassurance. Or it can simply get you thinking. It is also a way to differentiate your older self from the younger you. You can handle a search now that goes deep inside. You can appreciate the esoteric. You can see your connection to other things that may not have been visible to you before.

One purpose for growing older is to contemplate a larger view of the world. You are at a place where you can begin to put the puzzle pieces together. Do it for yourself, and don't be afraid to share your secrets with those who aren't quite there yet.

Chapter Eleven
Passing Your Secrets Around.

Several years ago I had an interesting conversation with a woman from Vietnam. She was talking about her teenaged children, and from the way she described them, they sounded extraordinarily well-behaved. I asked her how she was able to "train" them so well.

She laughed and said, "Since they were very young I have told them, 'I am your mother and I know much more about life than you do. Take my advice while you can. Someday you'll have to figure out the world by yourself.'"

I should've said the same thing to my son years ago. It was such an obvious but powerful way to describe the parent-child relationship: I know more about life than you. Take my advice now, because you'll need it when you're on your own.

Would this unadorned explanation of the way the world works have worked with my child? Or yours? Would it work with your grandkids?

Playing the wisdom card may not have popped into our heads when we were young parents. But it is one of the entitlements of growing older. As Jung pointed out:

"In primitive tribes we observe that the old people are almost always the guardians of the mysteries and the laws. . . [and this is how]. . .the cultural heritage of the tribe is expressed."[1]

He goes on to say, ". . .the wisdom of our old people. . .their precious secrets and their visions. . ."[2] need to be articulated and heard.

Ever since I entered my sixties, I've felt the need to pass my wisdom around. I'm not sure why I feel this way, but sometimes I want to save the younger people I bump into from self-inflicted stress because I see how overextended they are. Other times I just want to remind them that certain unhealthy habits (not getting enough sleep being one) can come back to bite them as they age. Do I sound like an old busybody?

Yes. I welcome the role. I always preface my gentle (I hope they're gentle) remarks to young people with my concern for them and with the reminder that I was once their age, and I know how they feel.

Which brings me to a rather impulsive conversation I initiated with three young women who were smoking on a patio behind a bar. They were not patrons of the bar but were taking a break from work.

The smoke was bothering me, but that's not why I said something to them. I saw three pretty, carefree women who could end up being three older, unhealthy, and maybe, burdened women who had acquired a lifelong habit they couldn't shake.

I think I said something like, "You look like such happy, healthy young women, and I'm worried that if your smoking becomes a habit, when you're my age, you're not going to be able to be all you want to be." I added, "Women my age who have smoked their whole lives can have lung and heart problems. And they look much older than they are." I had to throw in that last bit to get their attention.

You won't believe what they said. They actually appreciated my interest in them. Two of them piped up and said they were planning to quit. They all agreed smoking wasn't good for them. Then they asked me what the smokers looked like who were my age. (I told you the *looks* thing would hit home.)

You may not want to interject yourself into strangers' lives. I'm still surprised I did it. But inserting your wisdom into a conversation that warrants it is exactly what older people can do and maybe should do.

> *Like the moon,*
> *come out from behind*
> *the clouds! And Shine!*[3]

> Buddha

Take the Nama people in South Africa. They are known for exalting the wisdom of their elders. Older people in the Nama tribe have "high status" and "their advice is sought by the young" on social, political, and personal issues[4]. Aging Nama, my guess is, don't have to think twice about passing on their opinions to younger folks. Nama twenty-somethings undoubtedly pay attention.

Native Americans use the terms Grandfather Heaven and Grandmother Earth "to link the wisdom of tribal elders with the indwelling wisdom of the cosmos."[5] For centuries, and even today, elders in the longhouses of the Onondoga Nation preside over community matters, and chiefs defer to their wisdom.[6] Here's one older women are going to love: in pre-patriarchal cultures, it was the *crone* or wise woman who was honored for "her serenity and spiritual power."[7]

Wisdom and age have always been paired. We say things like, "He is wise beyond his years." When we picture a wise person we usually envision someone with gray hair and an older face. Is it because growing older brings on wisdom? It certainly can.

As Stephen Hall points out in his *New York Times Magazine* article on wisdom in 2007, ". . .an advanced age increases the odds of acquiring the . . .life experiences and emotional maturity that cultivate wisdom." Because "successfully coping with crises and hardships in life," as researcher Monika Ardelt (University of Florida at Gainesville) notes in the same article, is not only the mark of a wise person but "also one of the pathways to wisdom."[8]

A wise person is able to put situations into perspective with calm detachment. I've been here before, the experienced person thinks. I can deal with this. The wise older man or woman can approach a difficult issue as a "puzzle to be solved."[9] In the end, if the puzzle's solution remains fuzzy, the wisest advice can be to just let things go. Wisdom often means that everything doesn't have to be "fixed" and problems have a way of solving themselves. You know these things because you've been around long enough to get a sense of how life plays out.

Back in 1984 the Berlin Wisdom Project set out to see if scientists could get their arms around the often elusive concept called wisdom. Led by well-known quantitative psychologist Paul B. Baltes, the Berlin Paradigm, as it came to be known, defined wisdom this way: "an expert knowledge system concerning the fundamental pragmatics of life."[10] Kind of sounds like the definition of street smarts.

Jacqui Smith, who was one of Baltes's collaborators at Berlin's Max Planck Institute for Human Development, added that wisdom is "like peak performance. It's the highest level of potential or achievement that a human mind might be able to [attain]."[11]

Let that sink in for a moment. The highest level a human mind might attain. And the "optimal age" for wisdom, according to one paper published by Baltes's group, seems to be someone in his or her sixties.[12] The Berlin project, though considered controversial among some researchers, spawned other investigations.

Today researchers pile on characteristics linked to wise behavior: "reflection" and "compassion," notes Dr. Vivian Clayton, a geriatric neuropsychologist in Orinda, California.[13] Accepting "reality as it is, with equanimity," says Professor

Monika Ardelt, and she goes on, the wise among us "understand situations from multiple perspectives, not just their own," and they are tolerant.[14]

Wisdom means not only having your own emotions under control, but also tending to the emotional needs of others. It is about focusing less on what you "need and deserve" and more on helping other people, points out Professor Laura L. Carstensen, founding director of the Stanford Center on Longevity in California.[15] Sounds like a lot of grandparents I know. Maybe that's why kids love going to grandma's house.

Which brings us to the notion of the "first grandmother." We can't exactly point to one woman and say she was the world's first grandmother. But as William Thomas points out in *What Are Old People For?*, it's an intriguing hypothesis, because the "first grandmother" changed everything.

My guess is that when a prehistoric woman finally lived long enough to become a grandmother, that's when she, and maybe others like her around the same time, became instrumental in helping their grandchildren survive.

Thomas describes it this way: It was all a new mother could do to tend to her newborn. If food was scarce, the baby would get mother's milk. But the "first grandmother" was the one who found food for the older child, the first-born, and shared it with him or her. It was due, in great part, to the wisdom of the grandmother, Thomas asserts, that young mothers were able to reproduce successfully and grow their families.[16]

The caring behavior of this fledging grandmother allowed for millennia of future nanas and grandpas. What would we do without their counsel, we often wondered, when we were young parents? The reassurance of our own parents was important when we fumbled through the early days of parenthood.

How could grandparents remain so calm when our children were driving us bonkers? As grandparents ourselves, we have a better idea of what it means to be an unruffled presence when a two-year-old grandchild is in the throes of a tantrum. This elder "calming effect" is another article of wisdom we pass on to our children and grandchildren.

I remember when my son was a teenager, and my husband and I went to Chicago for the weekend. We decided to let my son stay home alone because he seemed to have the maturity to handle it, and he swore (on a stack of *Mad Magazines* or something) that he would have absolutely no one over while we were gone.

Saturday night comes, and my parents swing by our house to see if my son is lonely. They needn't have worried because the joint was jumping. All the lights were on, music was pouring out of the screened windows, and teenagers smoking cigarettes were everywhere.

While I probably would've screamed my head off and grabbed a few interlopers by the collar, my parents coolly steered everyone out the door. My dad then put his arm around my son and said, "You'd better pack your things and come home with us."

It turns out the party was more than my son bargained for, and he was relieved my parents showed up early in the evening. Later my son told me, "Grandpa was so nice, and I felt horrible for disappointing him." Who else but a grandparent would've had the wisdom to see that my child was overwhelmed and embarrassed by his inability to rein in the partygoers? Who else but a grandparent would have the good sense not to call us in Chicago and upset a romantic weekend?

> *Wisdom looks to see the jewel or flower*
> *shining beyond unexpected places . . .*[17]

> Spanish saying

Wisdom takes us beyond a black-and-white view of the world to the complex gray areas that make up much of our lives. When we are young we can't always see the most elegant solution to a problem, we don't always come up with a resolution that's in *everyone's* best interest.

But as an older person, we are more likely to be able to hold opposites and realize that situations we come across can't always be put in the "good" or "bad" column. They are nuanced.

An important tenet in the study of Kabbalah (ancient Jewish mysticism) is the concept of "holding opposites." "The Hebrew idiom designating paradox (*nesi'at hafachim*) means 'the lifting of opposites.'"[18] When we talk about wholeness, according to Dr. David Sanders of Kabbalah Experience, we are embracing "separateness, wholeness, and brokenness and all other paradoxes and opposites."[19]

It takes wisdom to be able to see that reality is a combination of all these things, that manifestations of separateness, brokenness, and wholeness reside in each one of us. That we can rise above light or dark and recognize life's sepia landscape.

> *Therefore having and not having arise together. . .*
> *Long and short define each other . . .*
> *Front and back follow each other..*[20]
>
> Lao Tsu, *Tao Te Ching*

One of the reasons Kabbalah study used to be reserved for people over forty was because it was believed only a mature person could understand a concept like holding opposites. But maybe the real reason was that only a wise person would recognize how this sophisticated principle played out in his or her own life.

I think it's hard for many of us, now that we're older, to think of ourselves as wise people. When I picture a wise person I always think of someone who is smarter and more gracious than I am. At the same time, my perception of life and of the people I interact with, or even read about, *has* changed. I find myself more likely to see how another person can think the way he does even though I may not agree with him. I see that what I perceive as shortcomings in others are very much like my own fallibilities. Humanness is a quality I am coming to terms with, in others and in myself.

It's been said that it takes ten thousand hours to master something. Knowledgeable Beatles fans know the meteoric ascent of their favorite band wasn't truly meteoric. The Beatles played scores of gigs in little-known venues all over Europe before their sound turned the rock world on its head. You could say John, Paul, George, and Ringo spent ten thousand hours becoming the Beatles. Think how many hours you've spent becoming a wise elder. In many ways it's been your life's work.

Perhaps you didn't recognize those shiny pieces of knowing when you picked them up through the years. You didn't think your accumulation of experience meant you were harvesting wisdom. But the universe seems to be set up that way: the longer you look at something, the more you can see it.

Nothing may be more valuable than your perspective. You can't buy it; there are no short cuts to getting it. It comes from the process of living and the repetition of life. The ups and downs of daily existence eventually sink in. Once you reflect on them, wisdom emerges.

What secrets would you like to pass on to others who may have a few years to go before they're elders? What life lessons have you learned, in your hours as a human, that could save a few young people some stressful moments? How can you open up yourself to wisdom still developing within you?

❰**Reflect** on the precious stones of wisdom
and learning you'd like to share with others.❱

What is the most important life lesson you've learned?

What would you tell your twenty-year-old self if you could go back and share your wisdom with him or her?

Which qualities in yourself have sustained you most as you've moved through the years?

If you had known thirty years ago what you know now, how would this knowledge have changed your life?

What important information about you and your family's heritage would you like to pass on to your children, grandchildren, nieces, and nephews?

(My son, in his late forties, finds our family history fascinating. He even likes looking at old pictures. Sometimes I pull out family albums on holidays so he can go through them. The trick is not to get carried away, which I could easily do.)

How do you measure a life well-lived? How can your older, wiser view of what it means to live well help younger people around you?

How can you be more aware of your own aha! moments in years to come?

If you could give one piece of advice to a young person today, what would it be?

If you're running out of secrets to share, here's one you can lay on millennials: someday they'll become invisible. Most young people don't know anything about the transparent quality we take on as we age, but you can tell them that one day when they're older, poof! they'll disappear. They will wonder what on earth you're talking about, but you can simply smile and say, "You'll see." Or they can read the next chapter. Better yet, read it with them.

Chapter Twelve
Now We See You. Now We Don't.

Two women walk into a bar. One is young, the other is you. Who does the bartender notice first?

The young one, because you're invisible.

It must be a phenomenon or syndrome or something. Because older women talk about it all the time, and they use the same word, invisible, to describe how they feel.

We're standing at the cosmetics counter, waiting to be waited on, and it's like we're not there. We're waving our hand in the air to ask a question at a meeting, and the speaker looks right through us.

How is it that when a woman enters her later years she seems to vanish from plain sight?

The answer, unfortunately, is simple: our society doesn't find her worth seeing anymore.

As our hair gets grayer in an ageist culture, our faces become more lined, and our shapes sag a bit, people think we're no longer a player. No, not *player* as in a guy who strings women along, but *player* as in someone who matters, someone who's part of the action, who has something interesting to say; someone who gets it.

We may think we're all of those things, but ageism has a way of spreading its dark wings over our everyday lives and invading almost everyone's psyche, including our own.

We're a visual society. We look at appearance first. Maybe all humans do. In our culture, though, we seem to put more emphasis on the physical presentation a person makes rather than on what's inside. It's a quick look, and we sum up the person in front of us. Young equals good, perhaps intriguing, someone we may want to interact with. Old equals not young, someone we don't want to interact with, who isn't interesting; maybe a little old lady we'd rather pass by.

We have to consider the reactions younger people have to us before we can come to terms with ageism and feel better about our older selves.

This is where the concept of loss comes in. Because it's at the core of how we feel about our progress toward old age. In some very obvious ways our losses are the reasons why younger people treat us the way they do.

The longer we live, the more loss we experience, which includes the loss of our youthful appearance. Though our culture is certainly over-enamored with smooth, young faces and skinny silhouettes, we do have to come to grips with the fact that we don't look like we used to.

My mother always told me that women look best in their thirties. Looking back now, I think she was probably right. Thirty-something women are attractive. They're no longer baby-faced but still young.

What are we supposed to do, though, when we're in our fifties or sixties, seventies and eighties? We have a lot of years left after we turn thirty-nine. Who wants to spend that time feeling as if we're sliding downhill into invisibility?

A number of older women and men don't care all that much about how they look as they age, but plenty of people of both sexes do. Maybe it's the guy who doesn't like losing his hair or a woman who has gained weight and can't lose it. How can we feel better about our own physical aging, particularly in a culture that values outward appearance so much?

If we are going to be kind to our aging selves, we need to face our losses.

The first step toward feeling good about how we look is to be realistic about it. When you glance in the mirror, what do you see? You don't have to be head over heels about everything that's there, but it is you, after all. Just an older version.

Try being objective about your aging self. Look at yourself as if you're not in you but observing you. "So this is the way I've aged. I can see how I've changed. Is it how I thought it would go?" You can be curious too, like you were when you were young and wondered what you'd look like all grown up. How will you age from here? What will you be at seventy or eighty? It can be interesting to speculate.

One reason I don't want to get a facelift is that I want to see what nature has in store for me. It's part of the span of my life—how I will outwardly grow old. What will I look like at ninety if I make it? I'm looking forward to seeing myself. The smile, those eyebrows that were always kind of thick—will they still be there?

I know a woman who doesn't like to look in the mirror. She specifically avoids it. The funny thing is, she's quite attractive. But when I asked her why she doesn't look in the mirror (how does she comb her hair?), she said, sotto voce, because I look old.

Well, you're seventy-three, I was thinking, and beautiful. I said, "Aren't you curious to see how your face and body are changing and will change in the future?"

She gave a little laugh. "I don't want to look too closely at myself because I'm afraid to see what's there," she said.

The changing, the metamorphosis. It's lovely to watch a pretty woman become more so, in a different way. I think my friend should welcome her reflection and be happy about what's there. She's seventy-three, in good health, and has a striking appearance. Isn't that what we're all hoping for?

Yet it is still okay to feel melancholy about our once-young faces and bodies. We have changed. We have lost something. It is hard to go forward and be content with ourselves without letting that soak in.

Oh, how we started out: unlined skin, no little bumps or veins popping up in unwanted places. A full head of hair. Yes, we were fortunate to experience being young. For most of us it was a sunny time, our lives ahead of us. Every day as a youngster was new with adventure, from our guileless point of view.

It's comforting to remember and feel fondness for our young years, to sit with these thoughts for a while. It's also important to acknowledge the sadness of youth's passing.

When we were young our bodies felt good. Strong. Not achy, like they do now. We've had surgeries since then, many of us. We've had to heal from broken bones or disease. We may be living with disease. It's all part of who we are. It's part of life. We have to take in what has been lost to us, feel it deeply, and console ourselves.

We need to let others console us too. Sometimes it's important to surrender to the love and care of other people. When we let go enough to receive help from those near us, we are more open to our own renewal. When we're lifted up by others, it's easier for us to see ahead to a better time, because what is weighing us down doesn't weigh on us so much. Even without articulating it, we may be able to appreciate that we're not alone.

No one ages without loss, including very healthy older people. There are losses besides the physical ones. The loss of a partner, parents, child, sibling, or a lifelong friend. To experience the losses the years have brought us is part of being alive.

Over time I have worn several skins,
peeled off, one by one, like husks . . .
some force is paring me down to the
marrow of what I must be.[1]

> Marcy Heidish
> "Changing Skin"
> *Where Do Things Go?*

Paring down may be part of the process of aging. Letting go of
parts of ourselves or of the people who were once integral to
our lives. Getting to our essence as we try to do with meditation or in our spiritual contemplation. Maybe growing older
is a winnowing exercise.

As we let go of the charm of youth, the quality our culture
holds dear, we find nature provides a balm for us to ease its
passing. It is perhaps a more valuable article than any allure
our younger selves ever had.

It's called resilience.

Resilience that begins with adaptation.

> "Old age may be a time of loss. . .but. . .There is a coun-
> tervailing and equally significant increase in the power of
> adaptation."[2]

> William Thomas
> *What Are Old People For?*

As we age we become "champions at letting go"[3] of difficulties, big and small, that surface in our lives. We are constantly redefining ourselves based on physical changes, among other things, and that's how we're able to adapt to our "new normal."[4]

Our new normal can include our older appearance, our fragile joints, or even something as fleeting as not bouncing back from a late night out. "New normal" can include profound adjustments—to disease, the loss of a job, or the loss of a loved one.

Resilience, in aging populations, expresses itself in many ways. Older people are not as quick as younger people to report feelings of depression. And they tend to have a greater sense of well-being than their younger counterparts.[5]

As William Thomas puts it, as we age, "the body instructs the mind in patience and forbearance" and at the same time, the mind shows the body how to be enterprising and flexible.[6]

> "The world's forever changing,
> and you just gotta adapt and evolve."[7]

> Eminem

I kind of like the idea of a new normal. It means we're "stepping up," redefining, once again, who we are. If the aging process is one of shedding layers (aspects of ourselves we don't need anymore) as Marcy Heidish suggests, then the new lean and mean you may be more suited to the older you.

It's fun, on some level, to make changes. Even when we're adapting to a condition we might not have wished on ourselves. We have new parameters, so we have to be creative about how we're going to function within them. Who are we going to be next? Are we actually stripping away our unnecessary parts in order to prioritize the most important parts of ourselves? Sometimes adversity, in an odd upside, can force us to do that.

Six months after my then ninety-two-year-old mother-in-law had her hip replaced, she was moving around pretty well. Then one evening one of her teeth fell out. My husband and I took her to the dentist the next morning, and the prognosis wasn't good.

Many of her upper teeth were in a precarious state, and the dentist suggested it was time to go to an upper denture and have her remaining teeth pulled. Six teeth in all.

Heavens, I thought, that's a lot to put a ninety-two-year-old woman through. My mother-in-law started to cry. I held her hand, and she asked for a Kleenex. The dentist referred us to an oral surgeon, and on the way home, Mom seemed to be shaking.

The next day I went to her apartment with some groceries, and she was full of good news. "I got a call to substitute for bridge on Monday," she said. "Now I'm back to playing twice a week. I'm so excited." She mentioned the impending surgery only once when she said, "If they put me completely out, I'll be fine. I just don't want to be awake when I lose all these teeth." The following day she was referring to her new "choppers" as if she couldn't wait for the dentures and her new normal.

Would I be so sanguine about having six teeth removed? How was she able to grieve over her loss so briefly and move on?

My mother-in-law adapted as only the very old can, would be my guess. She has always been a cheerful person, but I think after moving a number of times during her life, losing two husbands, and having her hip replaced, this was just another challenge to be met. She had handled other difficulties; she would handle this one.

Some say personality is 50% innate and 50% learned. My mother-in-law tends to be upbeat. She's also learned a lot about life. At ninety-four now, she has perspective few of us know. She has found out over the years that adapting to change has kept her spirits up. She has cultivated a reservoir of resilience, and she taps into it.

There have been a number of studies done specifically on resilience and growing old. In one study of one thousand adults ages fifty to ninety-nine, resilience was cited as "the secret to successful aging." The research team found that people with poor physical health but high levels of resilience rated themselves similarly to those with better physical health but a lower level of resilience. In other words, resilience helped people feel more content with their lives and their physical conditions. (Resilience was described as "the ability to bounce back from negative events or setbacks.")[8]

Though many older people are resilient, not everyone bounces back from adversity in the same way. Can we learn to build up a store of flexibility and sturdiness in ourselves? Will it help us be happier as we age?

Yes.

One way to foster resilience is to remember we already have it. We may not be aware of the personal stash of strength we've built up over the years, but it's there. Think back to all you've been through and learned about life. We don't give ourselves enough credit for just enduring a tough time, no matter what came out of it. Difficult experiences are always an opportunity to build resilience. "I've been through this before; I can do it again." This kind of thinking encourages older people to adapt and soldier through losses that come with aging.

Just thinking of ourselves as resilient is helpful too. When she was in her eighties, my mother would say to me, "I'm a tough old bird." At the time I thought it was an unflattering way for her to describe herself, but I don't think so anymore. She was old, and on many levels, she was tough. By saying those words to me, she was reinforcing her own hardiness. She was telling me she planned to survive. And she did.

But the end came for her as it does for all of us. Then it was my turn to buck up. I lost both my parents within seven months of each other, and I'm an only child. My parents were quite old, but for me, losing my entire childhood family in less than a year was devastating.

I had to spend more than a month away from home. I sold my parents' house, auctioned off most of their things, consulted with their lawyer over an incomplete will and problems with a hospital bill, wrapped up paperwork, and paid remaining medical expenses and taxes. It was a hard time because I didn't have much help. But what sticks in my mind the most is how incredibly sad I was.

How did I get through it? How was I able to function and be efficient when I felt so vacant inside? The memory of my rising to the task of settling my parents' affairs and dealing with their deaths reminds me that I have a reserve of resilience. I used it then and built upon it after that unhappy year.

I'm learning to be a tough old bird.

Acknowledging my ability to spring back means I'm changing my view of me. I see myself as a relatively resilient person at this point, though I can't pinpoint the exact moments when my grit kicked in.

Developing resilience and hardiness takes, first of all, a recognition that we have built a stockpile of it inside us from years of simply being alive. In addition we need to think of ourselves as experts in carrying on. We are experts. "Old people are survivors,"[9] as Dr. Andrew Weil put it in his book *Healthy Aging*. We didn't get this far without a bit of wherewithal.

We can also reinforce our sense of a good backbone by sharing stories of tough times with others. Hearing how other people handled their own difficulties encourages us to learn from them. Perhaps more significant, telling our stories of travail to a close friend, and hearing ourselves tell them, underscores our sense that we can, indeed, persevere.

I have a friend, Maggie, who lost her mother, then her sweet dog, developed back problems, and a few months later, almost lost her son. It was a difficult time for her, and she often told me how overwhelmed she felt.

But when Maggie's son became ill, she was determined to tend to him every day in the hospital. Committing herself to her son's recovery and physically being with him as often as she could gave her purpose. She was able to ride out her sense of being slammed by fate and helpless to stop it. Maggie developed a kind of witty irony over her trying year and a half. She seemed upbeat to me as she recounted tales, some jarring, some funny, of her hospital visits.

Happy ending: Maggie's son recovered, married, and is expecting a child. Maggie's back troubles went away, so to celebrate she adopted an older, handsome shelter dog.

The ancient Greek philosopher Epictetus makes an important point: "The thing that upsets people is not what happens but what they think it means."[10]

In other words, it's the spin we put on an event and our participation in it that affects how we view what happened. Maggie decided that her decision to "let what was meant to be, be" helped her cope during a stormy period. She feels good about how calm she remained through it all. I admire her.

I've decided that my ability to deal with my parents' deaths and the fallout and sadness that followed is evidence of my resilience and strength too. I could choose to dwell on some of the things that went wrong in the aftermath of their departing, but that would make me unhappy. And unhappiness is not my goal as I age. Nor Maggie's.

Being happy with yourself as you grow old is the point. Maybe it's time you took a moment to review all the wonderful ways you've survived tough circumstances and grown from them.

1. Think of a situation that was particularly difficult for you. What happened? How did you react? What did you learn about yourself?

2. If you've been through several tough times, reflect on how similar or different they were. What coping skills did you call upon with each experience? What do you tell yourself when you need to "rise to the occasion"?

3. Who do you know who is exceptionally strong and resilient?

   What abilities does he or she have that you can emulate?

4. How willing are you to change your view of yourself? Can you feel compassion for yourself as you've confronted challenging situations? Can you admire your ability to survive?

5. How would you describe resilience to a young person? What advice would you give him or her if he/she wants to learn to be more like you?

6. How often do you use your sense of humor when you're dealt a difficult hand? Do you have ways of calming yourself by drawing on a bit of lightheartedness?

We may be more likely to view our challenges with humor if we've been through a number of them. As we share stories of loss or struggle with one another, isn't it always encouraging when someone retells her narrative with a little wit and self-deprecation? It makes some of our direr times seem not so dark.

When we think of ourselves as resilient, that acknowledgment can make us happier with the process of aging. We see growth in ourselves, we find our troubles have been instructive, we've gained knowing and a certain mastery over life. Let's toast this happy occasion.

Which brings us back to the little matter of invisibility.

Now We See You Again.

You're in the bar, wanting to toast your forbearance and good humor, but you're still feeling invisible. You know you're mature, resilient, near the apex of your development as a human. But for some reason the bartender is still waiting on the younger woman.

Because you're probably wiser than anyone in the room, you realize you have sympathy for the bartender. He is a victim of our youth-oriented culture like everyone else. It's not his fault society is superficial. It's certainly not his fault that, as a people, we've forgotten how to grow old.

You smile indulgently, signal the bartender, and order a drink with an umbrella in it. You tell the bartender you're celebrating your age, that you're captivated by being sixty-eight years old, or whatever you are, and you've never been happier in your life.

He might ask you why that is, and you can entertain him with your philosophy on aging. Take your time enjoying your drink. When you go, leave a nice tip.

We have to start spreading the word somewhere, because becoming visible once more is not going to be easy. Society isn't on our side. We may not even be on our side. That's probably the first step toward feeling like we're worth seeing again: convincing ourselves.

We need to tell ourselves it's okay to reveal our age in every

possible way. We can't hide behind some faux-youthful image that is no longer who we are. We must reinforce to one
another that we deserve the attention of others. We expect to
be seen.

We know we're resilient. We know we have years of life experience and a mature perspective on the world. Our wisdom is invaluable, and we have to be willing to stand up for
ourselves as important members of the culture. We are not
mellow, sweet old people, as Maggie Kuhn put it. We can be
sweet and mellow, but you have to be respectful of us too.

First and foremost, we're players. Keep that in mind. And if
we're not convinced we're players, then we have to think like
the ancient Chinese philosopher Xunzi: We are a project in
progress. We can become new and better versions of ourselves, if we have a mind to.[11] We can hold sway as the elders
we rightfully are.

Once we let go of the stereotype of the Western aging man
or woman, we are free to be all the things we want to be in
our later years: wise and generous with our wisdom, eccentric, passionate about life, spiritual, sexual, resilient, curious,
playful, visible. It is hard for young people to be all these
things. But there is nothing holding *us* back.

It may take a while for the culture to catch up with our thinking. For the time being, though, let's view ourselves as prized,
advanced humans, the kind in everybody's visual field: un-
mistakable and well-acquainted with the world.

Now we see ourselves. Especially when we close our eyes.

You are in the desert. It's morning, and the air is dry but not yet hot. There are mountains in the distance, and nothing else is around you but soft sand and a few desert palms.

You are sitting, but you stand out, because you are you, at ease, presiding over this timeless place. You take a deep breath slowly. Into your lungs and belly. Then you breathe out, letting go.

You think of ancient people who have traveled this ground, and now you are another seasoned being who has been here too. The desert feels welcoming as you meditate, the elder in a land where the palms bow to you.

After a while you open your eyes again. For a moment you feel grateful just to be yourself at this time in your life. Which is good, because you may have to hold that thought for a number of pages to come.

Chapter Thirteen
Be Grateful, but Watch the Bonbons.

I'm going to tell you the bad news first: being grateful can make you fat.

A study published in the *Journal of Consumer Psychology* in 2015 found that when people were asked to express gratitude, they tended to crave sweets.[1] Apparently if you have to tell someone you're grateful, you think you deserve a reward, usually in the form of a confection.

This doesn't surprise me. I figured out years ago that being grateful was hard work. Like when you're a kid, and you ask for a new toy and your parents tell you to just be grateful for the toys you have.

That's when the antipathy begins. You're asked to show gratitude at the exact moment you're being denied something you want. You probably craved a Hershey bar and should've gotten one.

I think some of us started off on the wrong foot with gratitude. As kids we felt being grateful demanded a suspension of reality as we tried to feel something we didn't feel. What were adults talking about anyway? Now that we're older, we might still harbor a tiny bit of resentment when pressed to convey thanks. But maybe it's only when the person doing us a favor isn't doing much of one.

For the most part we do develop a better appreciation of gratitude as time goes by. Though people who suffer from depression, for instance, may have a tough time feeling thankful.[2] As Philip C. Watkins points out in his book on the science of gratitude, *Gratitude and the Good Life,* there are four other factors that can inhibit a person's ability to be grateful: "suspiciousness, indebtedness, envy and materialism [together, one factor], and narcissism."[3]

If you can overcome these difficulties, aren't clinically depressed, and are prepared to hold off binge watching TV with a box of bonbons, you may be able to feel and express gratitude to your heart's content.

What's so good about expressing gratitude? Almost everything.

First of all, conveying thankfulness can elevate your mood and make you feel better about yourself.[4] It can reduce stress, and in people with a history of depression, the process of writing down all the things you're grateful for can cut your future risk of depression in half.[5]

Gratitude helps you enjoy life more, makes you more popular, encourages your relationships, and even causes you to remember past events in a more positive light.[6] People who are grateful cope better with life's ups and downs.[7] In one study older people who expressed gratitude were less likely to be depressed over a financial problem than those who weren't as grateful.[8]

Philip Watkins, a noted researcher in the field of positive psychology and the science of gratefulness, defines gratitude this way: it is an emotion people experience when they believe "something good has happened to them, and they recognize someone else is largely responsible for this benefit."[9] Being grateful is something you feel and show to *someone else*.

You can be grateful to God if you are a religious person, that "someone else" being God. Or you can view the beauty of nature with a certain thankfulness, as one of Watkins's studies seems to suggest,[10] perhaps because nature can somehow be personified.

What about being grateful for you? Can you feel gratitude toward yourself? Dr. Watkins doesn't seem to think so, though I'm not so sure. Sometimes I'm grateful I did something or thankful I didn't. But maybe that's just relief.

The personality traits of grateful people, as defined by Watkins, are exactly what you'd expect: people who easily express gratitude tend to get along well with others and enjoy doing things for them; they're also cheerful, trusting, and compassionate. And they adapt well. Although, as Watkins points out, when it comes to defining characteristics of grateful people there are some "inconsistencies in the literature."[11] For the most part, though, it sounds like those who are thankful are the kind of people we like to be around.

Gratitude is the sign of noble souls.

Aesop

If grateful people have certain qualities we admire, what would happen if we showed more gratitude in our own lives? Would we develop more of these desirable personality traits too? It's kind of a chicken and egg thing. Does a likeable person tend to show more gratitude, or does being thankful dispose us to being more likeable?

It would seem that if we show gratitude more often, if we are aware of our feelings of thankfulness in certain moments, we might be more agreeable all the way around. Our sense of well-being will be manifested in almost everything we do.

Be grateful to everyone.[12]

Pema Chodron

Pema Chodron, an American Buddhist nun, spreads a gospel of compassion in the Buddhist tradition. She firmly believes that gratitude is not only appropriate in moments where thankfulness may be an obvious reflex, but it's appropriate and natural in all moments. She says that when we're grateful to everyone, it's "a way of saying that we can learn from any situation, especially if we practice this slogan with awareness."[13]

Awareness means opening up to being in the present. Pausing, in a momentary space of time, to feel, hear, see, smell, touch, and experience what is happening now. To realize we benefit from everything we do and everyone we interact with. As a result we learn what we want to be and what we don't. Each moment can be instructional. Each person, if we truly take him or her into our moments, can help us see ourselves more clearly. For that we can be grateful.

I have some bad memories of sixth grade. My parents moved across town, and I ended up at a different grade school for the second half of the year.

One of my best friends went to this school, and she promised to take me into her group of girlfriends once I started in January. But it didn't work out that way. I'm not sure how it all unfolded, but she turned on me about a week into the semester.

Today you would call it bullying, but back then I didn't know what it was or why this one girl, my former friend, was so unkind.

I felt lonely and victimized, and I had no idea how I would get through the rest of the school year.

Many days I pretended to be sick so I didn't have to be in the same classroom with her. She whispered about me, taunted me, pushed me around on the playground, and turned other girls against me. I did my best to keep a low profile and went off on my own during recess. I wondered if summer would ever come.

It did, and in the fall a junior high filled to the brim with students from a number of grade schools diminished her power considerably.

I think about that girl from time to time. Through the years, and after giving it a lot of thought, I've come to realize she did me a service. Because of her I was able to feel what it was like to be a pariah of sorts, to be alone, unhappy, and even afraid. She deepened my compassion for others who are faced with a similar sadness and isolation, people who are maligned or are underdogs. Maybe I wouldn't be quite who I am today if she hadn't made the second half of sixth grade miserable.

Am I grateful for her? I guess I am. It's hard to give her credit, but she did make a difference in my life. Pema Chodron is right: anyone can influence us and help us see the world from another perspective. Even the person we least suspect.

Who knows? After much passing of time, perhaps my troublesome friend has also changed.

> The real voyage of discovery consists not in seeing
> new landscapes, but in having new eyes.
>
> Marcel Proust

Now here's the good news: our ability to feel gratitude and other positive emotions does increase with age. It boils down to the limbic system, especially the amygdala, a primitive part of the brain that controls emotion. That part of us becomes less responsive to negative stimuli as we grow older and more receptive to positive information.[14]

Positive thinking doesn't always ensure gratitude, but it can lay the groundwork for it. That and a lifetime witnessing good times and bad make us more aware of good fortune when it comes along. This exposure, over years, allows us to be grateful for experiences that maybe didn't seem pleasant at the time.

As we age we are not only grateful for those who facilitate the good things that come into our lives, but we also have a better understanding of our dependence on other people.[15] When we're young we may think we're the only ones who can shape our destiny: I did it. I get the reward.

But with maturity we understand that what we do is enhanced by the actions of many people. Think back for a moment to the professors, friends, relatives, even casual acquaintances who helped you get through high school and college. Teachers guided you, friends taught you how to study, acquaintances lent you materials when you needed them, relatives gave you financial support. It's true in even our most mundane, daily rituals, we are dependent on others, and they are dependent on us.

When eating bamboo sprouts,
remember the man who planted them.

Chinese proverb

Gratitude is not a burden of indebtedness. It is a freely given acknowledgment. By recognizing those who have helped us with efforts grand and small—even some people we don't think deserve it—we take on yet another virtue: generosity. Our saintly visage is complete.

Michael McCullough, a professor at the University of Miami, and his colleague, Robert Emmons, University of California Davis, published a revealing study in 2003 in the *Journal of Personality and Social Psychology*. They found people who were grateful were more likely to give back to others. There was an uptick in volunteering and generous behavior and, another bonus, grateful people were more likely to exercise[16] (maybe to work off the chocolate).

Generosity has its own rewards. What is it that makes us feel good about ourselves and everything in the world seem right at that moment we do something for someone else? Is it a surge in endorphins? Is it something spiritual? It's a pleasantness that spreads within us, as if we have opened ourselves up to take in light or goodness, even though we're giving goodness away.

We could be engaged in a small act like holding a door open for someone carrying a lot of packages. It could be the commitment of volunteering once a week. Maybe it's just listening to a person on the bus next to us who wants to talk about something and needs to be heard.

Generosity may be an ancient action that links us to others, a primal prompt that helps us connect with people and demonstrate good will. Humans are social animals and showing gratitude and being generous can strengthen social interactions. But there is more going on here.

When you are in the moment with feelings of gratitude or acts of generosity, you are not only succumbing to emotions, you are also giving away a part of yourself. There is an endlessness about it. We may put limits on our expressions of gratitude or generosity, but in the instances of giving, at the instant we *are* giving, it can seem like warmth is pouring out of us.

Author Angeles Arrien describes it this way: "As gratitude grows out of love, its expression creates an opening through which increased generosity and good will can emerge."[17]

She points to the Persian poet Rumi:

> *Love is a flame that once kindled*
> *burns everything, and only the mystery*
> *and the journey remain.*[18]

Is it a manifestation of love that is tumbling out when we give of ourselves? It may not come across to us as love every time we respond to someone's need, but it's hard to explain away the bit of bliss we feel.

If we are going to be kind to our aging selves as we assert our right to grow old, maybe we should extend our generosity inward. Buddhists believe it is hard to show generosity to others if we haven't already been generous to ourselves.[19]

How, then, do you be generous to yourself?

You allow more breathing room in your day when you need it, pull back from too many obligations. You make yourself a cup of tea in the afternoon and put your feet up. You treat you as well as you treat the people around you.

The fundamental expressions of the age-old practice of Huna (Hawaiian mysticism) are described this way: "Loving yourself, nurturing other beings and the land, and living in harmony with all of life."[20] Followers of Huna keenly embrace generosity and gratitude: "When gratitude comes from the heart and is sincerely expressed. . .it sets up a strong positive vibration for the future."[21] That includes raising *mana* "in both the one who thanks and the recipient."[22]

Mana is at the core of Huna belief. The word means *energy* and is also described as "a spiritual power or vital life force."[23] Almost anything good that comes your way is a result of *mana*, something we can all use a little more of.

If gratitude is good for us, and generosity and even *mana*, for heaven's sake, flow from it, how do we engender more of it? How do we become more grateful and generous and anoint ourselves with happiness and good health? It comes back to awareness. We have to think about expressing gratitude and being mindful when we're generous. It isn't difficult, but it does begin with giving ourselves the same dose of kindness we extend to others.

❮Consider *ways to infuse more gratitude*
and generosity into your life. ❯

Make a list of the five people you're most grateful for. Then tell them how much they mean to you.

Are you grateful for some of the difficult experiences and demanding people in your past? What have you learned from them?

What are you most grateful for today? Write down anything that comes to mind. Make a habit of thinking about even the simplest things that evoke gratitude. It could be the sun coming through your blinds in the morning or the cup of coffee waiting for you at breakfast. See? You've perked up already.

Try to come back to a feeling of gratitude throughout the day. Make note of some of the good experiences you've had and the people who have been helpful to you. Remember those moments as you drift off to sleep. Write down a few of them now.

How can you be more generous to yourself? What can you do to treat yourself in a more loving way? How can you give the same care to yourself that you give to other people you love? Think of something you've been wanting to do but haven't fit in the time to do it. Be generous and allow yourself to have what you want.

Who could use more generosity from you? What small thing can you do for someone today that could make his or her life happier? It could be phoning or emailing someone who hasn't heard from you in a while. It could be inviting that person to lunch. Think of the euphoria you'll feel when you pick up the tab.

As we grow older we are able to look at life from the long view. The little disturbances that bubbled up every so often in our past have been smoothed down by time. The positive transmissions into our brains, say scientists, have increased with age. Gratitude and generosity flourish, sweet tooths aside. *Mana* is everywhere. Life appears mostly good, looking back, and it looks good going forward. Don't be put off by the drawing on the next page.

Chapter Fourteen

"You Cannot Be Serious!"

John McEnroe

You've had a nice life here, but I'm afraid your time is up.

That was abrupt. You're minding your own business, and then one day out of the blue, the guy in the robe (see previous page) pays you a visit, and you are no more.

Could this happen? Because in a tiny compartment of your brain you've always held out hope you'd be the exception. Sure, everybody dies, but when it came to your own end, somehow you thought you'd skate out of it. You couldn't picture the exact details of how you'd be spared, but you could never imagine yourself dying, either.

They say death is a part of life, but is it going to be a part of yours? The end of yours? You may joke about it, but mostly you don't think about death, because the whole thing makes you uncomfortable.

The Western response to death is something like tennis iconoclast John McEnroe's famous outburst at Wimbledon years ago: "You cannot be serious!"[1] His irate response was over a line judge's ruling on his serve. McEnroe couldn't believe any judge would call his ball out of bounds.

In a similar way, we find death an affront to our modern technology-can-trump-anything mindset. It is absurdly final in a way our daily diversions won't let us grasp. It's a ridiculous reward for a life of work, accomplishment, and the giving and receiving of love.

On a smaller, more personal scale, sometimes when we confront the death of someone close to us, disquieting emotions come to light. After the funeral we may feel vaguely relieved or even guilty it didn't happen to us.

We are far removed from the gritty facts of most human experience—the exotic diseases that infect much of the world, days spent growing food and fighting the whims of nature, drought and downpour. The flimsy barriers between inside a shelter and the outside, where chickens and goats wander onto dirt floors. Our Western life is sanitized. So is our view of death.

And look what materialized here: this chapter on death was supposed to be the thirteenth chapter in the book. Did I plan to link this superstitious, numerical marker to the subject? Or was I minding my own business when unlucky 13 popped up in an early outline of the manuscript? In the end I moved the death chapter to #14.

Maybe I didn't want to think about luck or superstition or death either.

This is what the real fuss over old age is about: admitting that death, preceded by aging, is a part of life. It's something our Western culture doesn't do very well. The waving away of death, the denial of it, is making the journey of growing older that much harder for you and me.

Now that you've figured me out, you're already thinking I'm going to tell you about societies where death is viewed differently from the Western vantage, where the end of life is out in the open, maybe even savored, and the comparison with our cultural backdrop is dramatic. You're right.

Transport yourself now to Indonesia. On the warm island of Sulawesi, where clouds, heavy with rain, sweep in briefly from time to time.

A half million Torajans live here. When they celebrate joyous events with their families, they don't necessarily throw elaborate, budget-busting weddings like we do in the U.S. Instead, on Sulawesi, they glorify life through spectacular funerals.

Funerals, like weddings, bar mitzvahs, and family reunions folded into one, are the "glue" that holds Torajans together.[2] A large majority of them are officially Christian, but their traditional Torajan religion, *Aluk To Dolo*, or Way of the Ancestors, still holds Torajans in thrall.[3]

Perhaps the most startling aspect of their devotion to the death of loved ones is the mummifying of them. This may cause us to question the thinking of the honorable Torajans. But their society, unlike ours, greatly prizes the process of death. They don't see death as the final cut-off point from life; they feel death takes place over a long period of time.[4]

Torajans believe their dear ones aren't actually gone when they die, and that death is "not a brick wall but a gauze veil."[5] This is why they house their dead, yet preserved, relatives in their own homes, dress them in finery, bring them food four times a day, and treat them with affection and deference, even though they are clearly not alive as they once were.

Torajans grieve for their departed kin, "but far from pushing death away, almost everyone . . .holds death at the center of life."[6] Death takes time, say Torajans. Those who are no longer living may not want to leave earth and their families too quickly. Immediate family members allow the departed the opportunity to move gradually on to the next life.

Looking at Torajan culture objectively, their obsession with death as a process and the preservation of dead bodies could be their way of comforting themselves when relatives die. It's not only about helping the dead transition to the afterlife, it's about giving the sorrow-filled family the space they need to reconcile the passing of someone close.

Grieving takes time. Maybe in the West we don't give ourselves enough of it to come to terms with the death of people we love.

I remember when my dad, who was near ninety, was undergoing intense physical therapy at a rehabilitation facility. We had brought him west to be near us and I visited him every day, as I did the Sunday before Labor Day.

Early Monday morning, on the Labor Day holiday, a phone call woke us at 5 am. My husband was downstairs and answered it.

As he came up the stairs to the bedroom, I called out, "What's wrong with Dad?" No one else would call so early.

My husband stood at the bedroom door. "He died," he said.

I couldn't hold that thought. For several moments the idea seemed foreign, so incomprehensible that I had to ask several times, "He died?"

When we arrived at Dad's room in the rehabilitation unit, his unmade bed was empty. His robe was on a chair. Dad was gone. I sat on the bed and cried. I lay down and put my face in his pillow. I kept saying, "Dad." I think I was shouting. I'm sure everyone on his floor could hear me.

We went to the funeral home, and Dad was already in some room in the back. It seemed strange to know he was there, but I couldn't see him or hold him or talk to him. I didn't think to ask. Dad wanted to be cremated, so we picked out a casket for the cremation. That was it. I never saw my father again.

We whisk away the dead. Even if we have a viewing at a funeral home, it's short-lived. The dead are there, and then they're gone. Best not to dwell on it. Get them in the ground or cremate them, so we're not reminded that death waits for each of us. And for each of those we love.

The Torajans may have the death thing figured out. Instead of seeing death as a stealth snatching-away of someone's life, Torajans are convinced it plays out unhurriedly. They give themselves room to indulge in their rituals of consolation.

It may take weeks or months for everyone in a Torajan family to gather together for the funeral. Afterward they still interact with their departed ones, talking to them, eating with them, including them in holiday festivals. When the family is finally ready to let go, they bury their beloved relative in an ancestral tomb.[7]

So, are Torajans dealing with the real world? You may wonder. Is their view of death based on what's physically happening to their loved ones? They think it is. As Robert Kastenbaum says in his book *The Psychology of Death*, "Truth itself. . .[is an idea] shaped within the cultural milieu and [is] best designed to function within that milieu."[8]

Then how does our Western view of death stack up? We think that when people are dead, they're dead. No pretending there is a "thin veil" between life and death. We would hardly prop up Grandma in the living room for months. And no one is suggesting we do.

But perhaps a more mystical acceptance of the end of life, some curiosity about death rather than so much foreboding, along with appropriate celebrations, could help us quell our specific, Western death anxiety.

Oh, death anxiety exists. Freud talked about it,[9] and psychologists, particularly here in the U.S.[10] and in other parts of the world, have studied it for decades. In the foreword to cultural anthropologist Ernest Becker's Pulitzer-prize winning book, *The Denial of Death*, Sam Keen wrote:

> The basic motivation for human behavior
> is our biological need to control our basic anxiety,
> to deny the terror of death.[11]

The fact that "U.S. psychologists have been especially active in death-anxiety research,"[12] according to Kastenbaum, is telling. Here in the West we, too, are subject to our own social and cultural influences. Death anxiety may be heightened for us because we try so hard to distance ourselves from it.

Human beings everywhere know they are going to die. Animals can voyage through life without the finality of death hanging over them. But how much do we, as humans, want to contemplate our own end? Is it good for us?

It depends on how old we are and how we do it.

As Kastenbaum points out, "older people in general do not report higher levels of death anxiety."[13] According to Robert Butler, they may fear death less than those in other age groups.[14] Besides, life's final work, says Kastenbaum, is to "accept the life we have led," (a superb reference to life review) "including the death by which it is concluded."[15]

Taking a cue from our psyches, then, these may be the perfect years to explore the mystery of life's end.

You may be on to something, you're thinking, but is it possible to make the contemplation of passing on a little more appealing?

I'm not afraid of death,
I just don't want to be there when it happens.

Woody Allen

Exactly.

This is a conversation we probably don't want to have with ourselves. Though it seems to me it's best to accept the reality of death, to hold death out in front of us and observe it. That way we can develop a personal philosophy about our own demise that will make us happy.

How can I put "happy" and "demise" in the same sentence?

Because the rationale behind this sentence may be the encouragement we need to tamp down death anxiety and ramp up joy in our lives.

As luck would have it, I've devised a three-point plan to address our unease. I'm feeling my way through this as we all are, but my plan leans heavily on religious and secular teachings from people who have been thinking about the unknowable over millennia.

Let's forge ahead with the following:

1. Death exists.
2. Death can be more to your liking
3. Death shouldn't mess with your head.

We survive. . .and then we die.[16]

   Ojibway elder

First of all, we should celebrate the fact that we survive. For the most part, we live lives that are satisfying and, at times, astonishing. In a way, it's hard to believe we've been privileged to live these lives for so many years. We're grateful for them.

Then we die.

So what is that? Many of us have "little personal experience with the death process,"[17] as Robert Butler pointed out in *Why Survive?*, meaning we don't live with the way death evolves, right in our homes, like we did before there were hospitals and hospice facilities. How can we describe death, then?

The medical definition goes like this: the cessation of all vital functions of the body including heartbeat, brain activity, and breathing.

   When you're dead, everything's wrong with you.

   Louis Armstrong

I think this bears thinking about. Not the "everything's wrong with you" part, but the cessation of life.

Being alive is thinking, breathing, feeling, absorbing, participating. Life is dazzling, stark, and relentless. Made up of good and bad experiences. Death is the absence of these things. Can we imagine nothing or being nothing?

According to some interpretations of Buddhist teachings, we *are* nothing. Before we were born we were nothing, though some may dispute that. The point is it's hard to imagine not being. But if we weren't aware of our existence before we got here, perhaps nonexistence isn't so frightening. It is our awareness that holds the fear.

Am I trying to talk myself out of being afraid? Maybe. But it makes me happier to think this way. Death exists. I've thought about what it means to not *be* anymore. When the moment of nothingness comes, it may not have the impact I worry it will. Because worry, among other things, will be gone.

If you are a person whose faith says that after death you will be aware of yourself, only in a timeless and more resplendent place, all to the good.

Are you cheered up? Not yet? Perhaps you will be once you read #2 of our 3-point plan: Death can be more to your liking.

All religions and spiritual philosophies address death with comforting words and rites. Through the centuries people have given the concept of not existing a lot of thought. Why not take advantage of some of their wisdom?

In Judaism there is a holy society called *chevra kadisha*. Pronounced hehv-rah ka-deesha. I learned about this beautiful concept from a friend who is a volunteer member. The belief is that the soul is in transition when a person dies. The society is charged with staying near the body until it is buried. Members perform a ritual cleansing and afterward sit with the corpse as the soul departs.

This idea is meaningful to me because I think one of the things we fear about death is that we'll be alone. If you know you will have the presence of a *chevra kadisha* member by your side after dying, it may make you feel better when you visualize your own end. And my friend told me there are societies that will perform this function for non-Jews. I may sign up.

Christians also believe the soul transitions after death. They pray for their dead loved ones, sometimes long after the funeral. Would it make you feel more content to know people are praying for you after you leave this veil of tears? Good. Then ask those close to you to do it, even if you're not a dyed-in-the-wool believer in prayer.

The prospect of someone thinking about you after your exit may be heartening. The more you can find solace in what you've planned for yourself after death, the better you will feel about this whole, mystifying business.

Talk about planning for death. You can take a page from Rabbi Zalman Schachter-Shalomi. The author of *From Age-ing to*

Sage-ing, and the founder of the Spiritual Eldering Institute in Philadelphia, Rabbi Schachter-Shalomi decided he wanted to experience death before he actually died. At least the after-death-ritual part. So, while he was very much alive he was attended to by a *chevra kadisha*, given the cleansing bath, dressed in a funereal garment, and put in a casket, presumably for a bit of time. I wonder how he felt about it?

Not long after his before-death/after-death experience, he died. Was he a little more familiar with everything after having gone through it? We'll never know. But if he felt more at ease before he died, contemplating his own passing after staging the rites, who are we to argue? Do what you need to do to come to terms with what lies ahead.

Sufis, mystics who are often Muslim but can come from many traditions, suggest that preparing for death is a matter of reflection and practice. Their advice is "Die before you die." Such was the rabbi's intention.

The Tibetan Book of Living and Dying sets out the Buddhist view of the life cycle in prose, poetry, and prayer. In it author Sogyal Rinpoche tells us that Tibetan Buddhists see, ". . .life and death . . . as one whole. . . death is the beginning of another chapter of life."[18]

He describes the philosophy this way: Reality is divided into four intertwined realms called *bardos*. They are "1) life, 2) dying and death 3) after death, and 4) rebirth."[19] Buddhists anticipate death by meditating on the *bardos* and understanding what they can expect once they die.

Apparently the more familiar you are with the *bardo* states and how to progress through them, the more smoothly transitions will go. *Karma*, too, figures prominently in the reincarnation metamorphosis. *Karma* is a Sanskrit word meaning "action."[20] Buddhists adhere to the belief that their actions in this life determine their future embodiment after death. Basically, if you are humane and compassionate now, you will be rewarded once you die and are reborn.

There is no doubt Buddhists think about death and prepare for it. Dying is central to their concept of life. You've lived before; you will again. The promise of having another life around the bend can be comforting from almost anyone's point of view.

> "I am just as certain as you see me here
> that I have existed a thousand times before,
> and I hope to return a thousand times more."[21]
>
> Goethe

Did the influential German poet Johann Wolfgang von Goethe believe in the Buddhist concept of death and rebirth? We don't know. But it appears he thought about something very similar.

You may like the idea of reincarnation. And you may want to factor this possibility into your own sentiments about death. Some people find the concept hard to imagine, but Buddhists gain peace from the expectation of death and rebirth. Maybe Goethe did too.

The Dalai Lama explains it this way: "I tend to think of death as being like changing your clothes when they are old and worn out, rather than as some final end. "[22]

As the reincarnation cards are dealt, your new state of being can even be influenced by "virtuous *karma*," he says, helping ensure a "happy rebirth."[23] It turns out you can guarantee a better future by being especially compassionate when death is imminent. If there is a modicum of control over any next state of our being, who wouldn't welcome it, no matter our take on the cosmic design?

Hindus, as we learned back in chapter ten, use their fourth stage of life to ready themselves for detachment from their current incarnation and prepare for a new life in the next. Because they are free from most familial and societal obligations, older Hindus can concentrate on their spiritual selves. They contemplate and meditate, reckoning with the end of life by cultivating a peaceful inner self.

You may already have firm religious views on death, but it's illuminating to discover how people of other persuasions see their own end. If you've adopted a death philosophy, there's nothing wrong with rounding it out a little and embellishing it to your liking. Your spiritual beliefs aren't there only for the sake of dogma; they are there to comfort you.

Last, and perhaps most important in our plan for a happy demise, #3: Death shouldn't mess with your head.

Shelley Kagan is an atheist. He is also Clark Professor of

Philosophy at Yale University, and he teaches a course on death. In his book *Death*, based on his course (a captivating skull on the cover), he writes that death is simply the end of life. Nothing to be frightened of. As Epicurus put it, "death. . . does not . . .concern the living or the dead. Since the former it is not, and the latter are no more."[24] Just the kind of thinking that would appeal to a philosopher.

Professor Kagan believes immortality (as many trust their souls will experience) would "be an unending nightmare."[25] The idea of living forever conjures for him an endless state of being that would eventually drive him nuts. Thank goodness (not his words) we die. "Death per se is not bad but good"[26] (his words). Because it brings us relief from too much "being." (my words).

He says while we can feel bad about dying too soon, our emotions "should be balanced by [recognizing] just how incredibly lucky we are to ever have been alive at all."[27] Death, in essence, is our rest, our nothingness after the intensity of so much something-ness, which is what it is to be living.

Finally, Kagan adds this: "death remains the ultimate mystery."[28]

Perhaps those are the consoling words we need to hear about our limited time. He is saying we have to coexist with life's most vexing uncertainty. We have to be okay with not having all the answers. Ambiguity is integral to living, and to dying.

Not knowing what will happen next is kind of the reason we

get up in the morning. What does life hold for us today? It seems appropriate to ask then, what will death hold in the end?

Most of the time we try to put a positive spin on what we do day to day. Why not put one on what happens when our days are over? How many of us know precisely where we will be in five years? Do we ruminate about it? No, we assume everything will work itself out. Borrow some peace of mind from the Dalai Lama and the Hindu in her fourth life stage. Let go.

Kafka noted, "the meaning of life is that it ends."[29] It's the living—what is going on in the sparkling present—that is important.

There's something freeing about letting go, agreeing there are things we can't completely know. It forces us to reside in the present moment. Just because we don't understand something after our many moments of living doesn't mean things will end badly. If Shelley Kagan, an atheist and someone who has given death a lot of thought, can be fine with the ultimate mystery, so can we.

To review: You recognize death and accept it as part of the life cycle of all living things. You prepare for your own end in a way that reassures you. And you tell yourself there are questions you just can't answer, so death doesn't mess with your head. That's it. That's the plan.

Can we have a little fun with death?

That's what an Irish wake is for. There aren't as many of them in Ireland anymore, but they used to be a way to lessen the sadness of a dear one's passing. Neighbors and friends would bring food and drink, sit with the body of old Uncle Seamus in the living room (sprinkling his corpse with whiskey), share stories with each other, and give comfort to the widow and her children.

When I was eight my Irish grandfather died, and his brothers and sisters came to his wake. My grandmother (who wasn't Irish) took to her bed with grief. But the oldest sibling, Aunt Nora, poured whiskey for everyone, and they told stories about their brother Jack. I remember the gentle recognition Aunt Nora extended me as she recalled Jack's irreverent humor. There was acceptance and ease and love in the room that October afternoon years ago, and I was part of it.

Celebrations of death are vehicles of consolation for family, but they are also a means to diminish the power of death for all of us. If we can open ourselves to respites of joy in the middle of our despondency, then our ability to ride through the labors of our own death may be buoyed. Maybe finality will seem more palatable because we've found bits of delight in some of its dark moments.

Who has more fun with death than the people of Mexico? The merry tradition of *El Dia de los Muertos* (Day of the Dead) at the beginning of November dates back thousands of years. Festivities, abundant with skull and skeleton images, take place in Mexican homes where it's believed the spirits of dead ancestors and relatives come to visit. Special altars are set up with food for the departed, and families camp out in cemeteries to commune with those who have passed on.

No one is afraid of dead spirits on the Day of the Dead. The observance is supposed to encourage a coming together of those who are alive and those who aren't. Do celebrants see the separation between life and death as a narrow one, not only on their annual holiday, but throughout the year? Have they developed a camaraderie of sorts with death?

Why do some cultures have an open, tolerant, even celebratory, response to dying while others do not? Why do some, like the Torajans, build an entire society around the end of life?

We can learn from them, if only to realize that our attitudes toward death can be fluid, and we can cast them in a way that makes us feel better about our own passing. We might even influence our children to see their old age and demise differently. Maybe we can enlighten them as we adjust our view of the life cycle.

How would you like to change the way you think about death?

❮**Fashion** *your own death view. Rethink it or enhance it.*❯

What do you fear most about death?

Are your fears about death similar to your fears about old age? Does either center on a loss of control?

Have you been with someone close to you when he/she died?

What were you feeling during those moments?

How have you been able to comfort someone who was dying?

In what ways would you like to be comforted when you are close to death?

Have your views about death changed as you've aged?

Are you more accepting of death now or less so? Why do you think that is?

Do you believe in an afterlife? Does this belief make death more acceptable to you?

Do you think, as Shelley Kagan does, that it's okay to die and cease to exist? What would that be like?

If you could choreograph your own death, how would you like the end to come? Who would you want to have by your side?

Have you thought about the meaning of death in your life? Have you developed a death philosophy that reassures you?

Have you talked about your philosophy with your partner, your children, or a friend? Why not?

How could you rethink your view of death so you would have more peace of mind?

What rituals would you like performed during and after your death?

Could you borrow ideas from other cultures that would enhance your acceptance of death? Why not?

How can you better live with the mystery of death and let go of thoughts that make you unhappy?

Would a more positive view of your own death affect your outlook on aging?

How would you change our culture's take on the end of life?

We think more about death now because the time ahead of us is shorter than the time behind us. This seems obvious. But what if we could look at *time*, the key element to our longevity, in a different way?

What if I told you we could manipulate time so it almost stands still? Or what if I said time doesn't exist at all? "You cannot be serious!" you'd say. But Einstein thought about this, and he was pretty serious.

Here's where it gets good: we can agree to disagree with the commonplace assessment of time, as we can with conventional views on death. But we can also look at time in a way that is more open-ended than we've seen it in the past. As you're about to find out, like Einstein, we can learn to be enchanted by time and space and beginnings and endings, including our own, in a universe that bursts with mystery.

Chapter Fifteen
Time is on Our Side.

I ndulge me for a moment while I explore the theory of relativity.

Stay with me here.

I'm not talking about diving into equations, I just want to reference part of the theory, the connection between space and time. According to Albert Einstein, both are bound up in one continuum called space-time. Why is this important? Because there's a fly in the continuum. And it's this: space and time may not exist.

It turns out scientists, over decades, have been toying with a concept called non-locality. To put it simply (so I understand it), the idea is if you separate two particles and place them at opposite ends of the universe, they act as if they're one particle. They behave as if there is no time or distance between them.

How do they know to do this? How can two particles worlds apart appear to be, not in two locations, but one? The truth is that no one is sure how particles pull this off. But in countless physics experiments too sophisticated for me, this phenomenon has been observed over and over again for years running.

Here's the upshot: "Many physicists now think space and time are doomed—not fundamental elements of nature [as we've always thought], but products of some primeval condition of spacelessness."[1] In other words, if the rogue particles are to be believed, space and time may not be real.

When I first read about this theory I thought, wow. This is heady stuff. It means that the universe we think we know (the one we learned about in school), isn't what we thought we knew. If space and time aren't there, what *is* there?

Einstein called this non-locality hypothesis, "spooky action at a distance."[2] He wasn't keen on two particles acting like they weren't where they were supposed to be. Though he tried, Einstein could never disprove non-locality. He figured that if time and space were nonexistent, there goes his theory of relativity, to say nothing of the laws of physics. Or words to that effect.

No one has given up on Einstein or relativity or physics. But today thinkers question the concepts of space and time as we have come to understand them.

What does "spooky action," then, have to do with reclaiming our right to grow old and being happy about it? And what do we have to do with Einstein?

First of all, I think it's fun to contemplate the big questions as we age. Now that we have the time, pardon the expression, we can fantasize about our quirky universe and what it means to be part of it.

If we ponder what's out there, even from a layperson's point of view, we also elevate our intellectual and spiritual journeys. Are there new meanings to the universe? How can I incorporate scientific discovery into my feelings about the cosmos? What is the takeaway for me, both in mind and spirit?

Another reason "spooky action" is germane to aging is that it gives us a new way to look at time. It has particular implications for people who are rooting for more of it. It's discouraging when we think about time as simply the measure of years we have left. It might help if we viewed the entity known as time from a much brighter perspective.

How would Einstein feel about this? I think he would tell us to go for it. He delighted in looking at ideas through an unconventional lens. He wrote a famous essay in 1936 in which he said that the amazing thing about the universe is not that we can't understand it; it's that we understand it at all.[3]

He didn't live to see non-locality come of age, but he could appreciate the unwinding of the mystery of time and space. I think he'd encourage us to think about it too, even if we're not physicists. Looking at time from a new frame of reference, not just the "spooky" aspect, but from a view with more practical applications, may appeal to the little Einstein in all our brains.

Life is short. Life is long. Life moves too quickly; life doesn't move quickly enough. Inside it can seem life hasn't moved at all. So many ways to look at time; so little time, in the scheme of things, to look.

Shall we deconstruct time? Let's pretend we don't know anything about the subject for the sake of exploration. Here's what Tolstoy had to say about internal time, how he felt about himself as an older man, looking from the inside out.

> ". . .I am conscious of myself in exactly the same way now, at eighty-one, as I was conscious of myself, my 'I', at five or six years of age. . .Consciousness is immovable. . .If time moves on, there must be something that stands still. . .my 'I' stands still."[4]

His "I" had never changed. Tolstoy believed the person who lived out his life inside was timeless. It was still the five- or six-year-old child who hadn't grown up.

Don't most of us feel that way? Who is the person who is happy or sad? The person inside you who is in love, lonely, worried, scared, relieved, joyful? Is it a child? A young adult? Many of my friends say it's the twenty-year-old they used to be or the child they once were. Time stopped somewhere, and the "me" inside, the "me" they say who looks out on the world, is that young self without the sensation of time having moved on.

What does this say about internal time? That it doesn't go forward as we age? That even though we learn, mature, and change, for the internal, emotional self, time doesn't exist? I wonder how old the internal Einstein was. Did time stand still for him too?

We have to admit that in certain circumstances time is timeless.

What causes our internal clock to get stuck in a youthful warp? Some believe the "I" that never changes is the eternal "I," the soul. Dr. Andrew Weil, physician and advocate of integrative medicine, calls this "I" our "unchanging essence."[5] He says it is the "spirit, the nonphysical core of our being."[6]

Others contend our early impressions determine how we see the world. We still see the world, or *feel* the world, from a young perspective. No matter how old we are, the youthful observer prevails.

If something inside us feels time is suspended, why do we have the impression it is roaring by? Whenever someone says, "Life is short," we tend to agree. We use the brevity-of-life excuse to justify all kinds of behavior, from splurges on vacations, to upending our careers to find meaning in life, to marrying someone impulsively. Some of these things are good. I don't know about marrying on a whim.

But we do have an imperative to move our lives along, especially as we grow older. This isn't time on the inside, but external time, what we sense all around us. Is life short? It depends on how we view it.

Compared to the universe, our time on earth is split second. Here one day, gone the next. But we could say the same about stars. They're here one day, then they burn out or get sucked into black holes. There are no guarantees in deep space, either.

All is relative. For instance, life seems to race by faster as we age because "a year is a significantly larger part of the life-time of a six-year-old than it is of an eighty-year-old."[7] On the other hand, it would seem our experiencing the novelty of the world as a child would make time fly by then too. Particularly if, as an eighty-year-old, we're spending our days rocking on the front porch, which could slow time down considerably.[8]

The idea of slowing down time isn't a bad one. Despite our feeling that time is racing by, it may be older people who ultimately help everyone else ease up, as Marc Freedman indicates in his book *Prime Time*.

Unlike people in middle age, elders have a different ap-proach to the hours in their days. They don't need to move at a frenetic speed to keep their careers afloat, so they can slow down to cultivate "relationships and the expression of care."[9] As Freedman says, the "expanding population of third agers may be precisely the counterbalance society needs"[10] to keep our values in check. Elders can become "the new role mod-els for balanced lives. . .[as the] virtues of slowness begin to take hold in the wider culture."[11]

In *The Second Half of Life*, author Angeles Arrien observes that now that she has time to linger at her kitchen table in the morning, everyday objects attract her eye in ways they hadn't before. A crystal salt shaker takes on prismatic beauty, glittering in the sunlight. She sees it as if for the first time, though it's been in front of her for years. In the past she was "just too busy getting things done" to notice what surrounded her, especially things she took for granted. She asks herself, What else have I missed in life because I was too busy?[12] What have we all missed?

It's hard for younger people to reflect on what they're missing if they don't have time to reflect. Our culture certainly doesn't give us much encouragement to take in the bigger picture.

In years past, when we used to sit in the park at lunchtime munching on a sandwich, we spent the time people watching or letting our minds wander to issues of the day and aspects of our lives. Now we're checking our phones.

In Teddy Wayne's *New York Times* article "The End of Reflection," he asks, ". . .are we eliminating introspection at times that may have formerly been conducive to it? . . . is the depth of that reflection compromised because we have retrained ourselves to seek out instant gratification . . ?"[13] How much is our culture affected by our addiction to devices? "The Internet typically rewards speed over all else, a quality at odds with deliberative thought,"[14] writes Wayne.

If we had more time to think things through, would our reactions to our friend's tweets or even to events in our world be more measured? Would we say something or end up thinking something far removed from our first reaction? Our discourse at times is coarse. Maybe because we don't give ourselves the time to work an issue through.

Here's where the older among us can be helpful. Many baby boomers didn't grow up with electronic devices. We didn't even have telephone answering machines. Some of us shared phone party lines and had to wait for others to get off the line before we could dial a number.

Because of our Pleistocene upbringing, perhaps we're not as attached to our smart phones as our more developed counterparts. We can be the ones to show younger friends the joys of putting down this electronic yoke from time to time and then responding to the world after considering it.

There are certainly boomers who do want to be connected 24/7. A number of older people are caught up in the whirl of moving lickety-split. They think if they slow down they'll miss something. Or if they don't keep up a frantic pace, they're proving just how old they are. Yes, they are proving that. They're confirming that wisdom and years have taught them life is to be appreciated. Time will slow down if you let it.

Is there anything worse than arriving at the airport early in the morning and finding out your flight's delayed? For hours? All of a sudden time isn't skittering past. It has come to a dead stop. There are moments (or hours or days) when time simply won't go fast enough. The last thing you need is to slow it down even more. Isn't it funny how time can move fast, then slow or even seem to stand still within a relatively short amount of, if you will, time?

That's one cool aspect of time. It can manipulate us or we can manipulate it. Depending on what we're doing or being, or whether we're caught up in our internal clock or an external one, time can be experienced in many ways.

You want to extend your time at this point in life? You want to slow it way down? There are methods, dear reader, that don't involve delayed planes.

About twelve years ago I came into my stress-reduction class feeling stressed. For one thing, the class was about a half hour from home. For another, I had to drive through rush hour traffic to get there. On top of that, it was close to dinnertime, and I was hungry.

So the instructor offered each of us a raisin. Not much of a snack. But she said mindfulness was a way to reduce stress. She told us we were going to eat our raisin and focus only on that. We were going to be mindful and strictly in the moment with our raisin. We were going to experience a raisin in a way we never had before.

First we looked at the raisin. Then we smelled it. What did we see? Did it have an aroma? We took our time.

Then we tasted the raisin, just a very small bit of it. We chewed slowly. We closed our eyes. Could we describe the flavor? Compare it to anything else? Was it sweet, a little sour? Both? What was the texture? How did it feel to chew a raisin? We ate the rest of it. What was it like to swallow our raisin? Did the taste linger? Did it change as we ran our tongue over the surface of our teeth? Did we like the raisin?

I'd never felt so intimate with any food in my life.

But I will say this: time stood still when it was just me and my raisin. When I was mindful of what I was doing, and in the absolute moment with my raisin, I wasn't aware of anything else. I couldn't get over how calming mindfulness was and how eating a dried grape brought the clock to a standstill.

Ram Dass calls this enchantment "the timeless present."[15] When we are at one with what occupies us, when we are truly in the present moment, with no thought of what happened a few seconds before or what will happen next, *"there is no time."*[16]

But isn't time still moving? you're wondering. Ask the physicist who studies non-locality. Whether time is moving or not, in a way it doesn't matter. It's how we *feel* time in our lives that is important, and we can learn to feel it differently. Nature has a way of letting time roll out in a constant flow of beginning, end, and beginning again. Think of the seasons or picture a river cutting through rock and forming a canyon. Elements wear down the canyon, the river dries up, and the process begins again. There is no timetable. The seasons aren't in a hurry. The river isn't impatient. They simply are.

When we are, when we take each moment as it comes, time takes on an endless quality. Remember our discussion of *flow* in chapter five? Mihaly Csikszentmihalyi talked about immersing ourselves in an activity we find so captivating that we literally get lost in it.

He adds this about flow and our awareness of time: "During the *flow* experience the sense of time bears little relation to. . .time as measured [by]. . .the clock."[17] He expands, "Freedom from the tyranny of time does add to the exhilaration we feel during a state of complete involvement."[18]

The tyranny of time. That's when time manipulates us. We fall into its slots. There is so much time for reading the paper or even baking a cake or taking a walk. Do we have to schedule our lives so tightly that time becomes the master? Now that we're older, can't we take the reins of our day and indulge in pursuits (like the ones that bring on *flow*) without a deadline?

Does it matter how long it takes to read the paper? If we decide to make a complicated cake recipe, who cares if it takes the entire afternoon? If our brief walk turns into an excursion of several hours, it might be fun. Our goal is what Lewis Richmond, a Zen Buddhist priest, calls "vertical time," a slice of time that pinpoints the moment. He relates this kind of time specifically to meditation, when we are most aware of our body and breath.[19]

As older people, we can extend this sense of vertical time. I think we can expand the moment at will. We can be in charge of time by letting go, getting into *flow*, meditating, among other things, and allowing desire to take us where it will.

As Margaret Cruikshank reminds us in *Learning to Be Old*, "Practices that change our relationship to time help us become aware that busyness is often self-inflicted."[20] It is. After all, we make our schedules, and we're the ones who insist on sticking to them. Sure, if we say we're going to meet someone for lunch, we need to show up and on time. But we don't have to rigorously portion out our days so events are blurred, not adsorbed, and our calendar is full because our culture says it needs to be.

If time can work for us and not against us, if even physicists say time could be illusory, then how do we get time on our side? What behaviors can we adopt to extend time or make it seem to stop altogether?

Jon Kabat-Zinn in *Wherever You Go There You Are* recommends this: "Think of yourself as an eternal witness, as timeless. Just watch this moment without trying to change it at all."[21] It's part of letting go, a way of life we can begin to practice.

Next time you're in line at the grocery store, instead of worrying about how long it will take to check out, observe what is going on around you. Look at the people, the groceries you're about to buy as you take them out of your cart.

Think about how fortunate you are to be able to put food on the table. Be a witness, in the moment, to other people, your surroundings, and your place in it. You may experience a calmness and suspension of time. This "witnessing" of life and pleasant slowing down of time can be translated into other parts of your daily routine. Even to the most mundane.

As I am writing, it is summer. The sun is hazy, and there are light clouds over the mountains. When I look up from the computer and out the windows, I see tree branches below me barely able to lift their leaves in the heat.

The park across the street is green and brown and empty of people. A wasp is bouncing against the window screen. The afternoon is subdued. Because I am watching the world around me, not expecting anything from it, and it's not expecting anything from me, there is a timeless quality to it.

Can I say this pause and observation evokes spiritual feelings in me? Thoughts I might not have if I weren't in my own Hindu-like third stage of life? If we are exploring our inner selves as we grow older, it seems appropriate that we are able to bring more eternity into our lives. That we can feel endlessness around us. As we witness time, elongated in front of us and stretching out far behind us, we see ourselves on that dot that is the very moment of the present. The moment that by its nature pauses time.

Being in Csikszentmihalyi's *flow* can have the same effect. We need to find more space in our days for who it is we love to be. A quilter, a collage-maker, a baker, a photographer, a guitar player, an amateur actor, a birdwatcher, a swimmer. Being in any of the roles we enjoy slows down time. We allow ourselves to get lost in an almost gleeful way. We are removed from giving the clock our undivided attention.

Certainly meditation, as we have seen, can hold time in check. It takes us away from the external to the place inside where we are still and time appears to be too. You can go there now, if you'd like.

Envision a planet so distant from earth that it seems separate from our own universe. It's a livable place, and just by willing yourself, you are there, sitting in warm light on its surface, looking up at the black sky. You feel comfortable and safe.

You begin to meditate by breathing in and slowly exhaling. You relax as you follow your breath, in and out.

You know the cosmos is filled with objects made up of the same material as you. You feel a connection to flickering stars above and below. They and all ethereal stuff have always been here, in one form or another. So have you.

In this timeless emptiness there is no before or after. There is just you, meditating now, in the present. Hold this peaceful thought.

The single sound is the faint inhale and exhale you hear as you focus on your breath. Allow yourself to go deeper into the quiet as you sit, untroubled, on your planet. Stay here awhile.

After many moments, you have no idea how long, gradually bring yourself back across the distance (or non-distance) of space. Over what may be millions of miles in a matter of seconds, if those who embrace non-locality are correct. In no time you are reading this book again, on your sofa.

You feel calm but awake, and your mind is rested. Which makes this the perfect opportunity to call up your creativity and figure out how to make time do your bidding.

❰Imagine *putting time on your side.*❱

Let's start with thinking about your internal "I." How old is the person who sees the world from inside you, looking out? Is it the six-year-old you? The twenty-year-old you? How does it feel to experience life from a timeless self? Why do you think the "you" inside doesn't age?

If the person inside you is timeless, what other aspects of your life aren't marked by time? Your memories? Some of your emotions? In what ways has time *not* affected you?

Do you often feel you don't have enough time in a day?

What would it feel like to have time at your disposal?

Are you afraid if you don't fill your time, you're not living up to society's expectations? Your own expectations? Are you afraid too much time would mean too much reflection? Are you worried that you'll have to think about where you are in life? About your own old age?

What kind of reflection would be most meaningful for you? What kind would actually bring you joy? Why don't you reflect more often on what makes you happy?

How can you infuse more mindfulness into your life? Are there moments when you can turn off your phone, close your computer, turn away from TV, and just rest in what's happening now? Can you try to eat with more mindfulness or exercise at the gym with your mind on your body and not on the clock?

When you're mindful, how does the passage of time *feel*? Do you have any sense of time at all?

Can you visualize timelessness? Use this vision (a beach, a mountaintop, a sunset, a planet in space) while you meditate. How can you get more meditation time into your life?

What activities are most helpful in slowing down time for you? How can you be in the role of the timeless self more often?

Are you familiar with the "many-worlds interpretation?"[22] I find this concept almost spookier than non-locality. It's the idea that parallel universes exist.

According to some scientists, there's a world (or worlds) out there just like ours. In fact, there's another *you* out there, or maybe several of you in that world or worlds. I'm not making this up. Physicists who believe in parallel universes say this is one explanation for the phenomenon of non-locality.[23] There's a movie script here.

Anyway, if I'm also in another universe, maybe I've finished writing this book. Maybe we didn't need this book in the first place because people in that other world already feel good about aging. They are honored as older people, their children understand them, and their grandchildren behave.

Back in our universe, though, we have work to do. In the next chapter I'll try to channel my duplicate self, whether space and time separate us or not, and move our right-to-grow-old paradigm forward. Are you and your other you with me?

Chapter Sixteen
Bucking the System. One More Time.

I was in ninth grade, and we were taking instructions on how to "duck and cover." You were to crawl under your desk, wrap your arms around your head, and wait for the all-clear.

We were preparing for nuclear war.

It was October, gray and chilly, and trees had lost most of their leaves in our suburb outside of Detroit. Because of its big industrial output, Detroit, auto capital of the world, was said to be a target of Soviet missiles in Cuba, aimed at the United States. People thought warheads could launch any day.

There was a feeling in my junior high that we had come to some sort of end. Not only were we shaken during the days of the Cuban Missile Crisis, but we had no surety about anything being ordinary or dependable. We understood we were the first generation to face the possibility of the end of the earth, destroyed by atom bombs. I think our fears swept aside everything else we were concerned about in October 1962. It was wild, new territory for teenaged baby boomers, but not in any good sense. Maybe that's why we rebelled so much later on; that and the Vietnam War several years afterward, when many young men my age were drafted into a conflict few appreciated.

Some say our generation was pampered and self-absorbed during the upheavals of the sixties and early seventies. I say not so. Nuclear threats held sway over everyone back then, and they were especially frightening for us, young people whose lives hadn't even gotten off the ground. I also remember how far removed my friends felt from the battles in Southeast Asia. Film on the nightly news could be terrifying. What were we doing over there? Yet our leaders continued to send us.

We did what we could to try to change the thinking of those in charge, people who seemed cavalier about annihilation of populations in other parts of the world and of the world itself.

We were not easily placated. We disrupted the status quo, supported civil rights and women's rights. We argued over war and values, and now we still have strong opinions about what we want going forward. Those who were children in the mid-twentieth century don't agree on everything at this point, but we have participated in and lived to see great change. I don't think we're finished.

Today there are one hundred million people in the U.S. over fifty,[1] and the bulk of them are baby boomers. We are once again that magic number that can tip transformation.

The Buddha said,

No one saves us but ourselves.
No one can and no one may.
We ourselves must walk the path.

As you may suspect, we elders, we baby boomers who were primed by an early brush with nuclear extinction, are not going to settle into our next life stage without a lot of consideration. What is it we want from the years to come? Can we remake the later days of the human life cycle into time that is significant and happy, not only for us, but for those who follow?

If we expect society to take our aging generation as seriously as it takes others in their life stages, then we are fortunate to be surrounded by ourselves. We already question many of the tired, cultural bromides used to mollify the old. We know we don't have to Defy Aging! if we don't want to. We don't even have to age gracefully. Our sizable contingent can set in motion a new age that encourages natural and pleasant approaches to the years that are waiting.

As we've noted, many in and surrounding the fields of gerontology are already on board with new thinking about aging, and a shift in rationale has started to take place. We are the ones to move it along. But everything depends on how much we want to buck a system that holds older people back.

Ram Dass says this:

"We suffer because of a desire, an attachment, a clinging... the more desires I let go of, the freer I become."[2]

This is important: We have to ask ourselves honestly if there is something that still keeps us attached to the current, constricting view of old age. How familiar, and therefore oddly comforting, is this burden of a slog we're expected to take through aging stereotypes? How much, even unconsciously, have we bought into the society-wide drive to maintain everlasting youth?

Are we part of the problem? As long as we join in the diminution of the older class of which we are a part, we aren't helping each other.

A young woman made a wise comment to me several months ago. She said women who get facelifts are not only saying there is something wrong with them the way they are. They're also saying there's something wrong with *every* older woman. (Meaning facelifts, according to the women who have them, should be *de rigueur* for everyone.) The minute we decide for whatever reason that we're not "good enough" as we grow older, we're tacitly making the same judgment about every other aging person.

We cannot allow ourselves to be our own worst enemy.

It turns out my gym is a swell place to hear older people berate themselves for being old. It's as if they're looking for like-minded compatriots who also see workouts as battles with a most precious enemy: their aging bodies.

The other day one of my gym friends said to me, we've got to find another word for *old*. He hates the word. A lot of people do. Yet I've heard my friend drop the "g" bomb (*geezer*, which I think is worse) when denigrating himself.

Why do we do this? Why do we always make the concept of aging, and all the words surrounding it, pejoratives, even when those words apply to us? By continuing to reinforce the idea that the word *old*, in particular, is an unspeakable term, we all suffer.

The next time you're about to whisper to a friend, "Does this dress make me look old?" why not say, "Does this dress make me look good?" That question takes *old* right out of the conversation and puts it where it belongs: in the realm of something you and your friend already acknowledge.

We are old, or in varying degrees of old-ness. What's wrong with that? Aging is not a problem that needs some kind of solution, as Thomas Cole points out in his essay, "The 'Enlightened' View of Aging."[3] Aging is a natural consequence of being human, of living. We are fortunate that many humans now live long enough to enjoy their own version of the Hindu third and fourth stages. We should be happy our bodies have taken us this far.

The time has come to make the leap from adulthood (as William Thomas defines it in *What Are Old People For?*) to elderhood. We're not listening to The Who back in 1965, when we believed it was better to die than get old.[4] We've rethought that.

Can we break away from our discontent with aging?

First we have to recognize that modern, mainstream culture has rejected any belief in natural aging. We are so far afield from the ancient concept of elderhood, a mantle to be sought after and enjoyed, that we even disparage the word used to describe what we are becoming.

We need to see how this thinking works against us. How can we possibly be at peace with old age if people, including ourselves, either recoil from the very thought of it or don't admit aging exists? Even new, scientific definitions of successful aging have a tough time breaking through our anti-aging prejudices.

Ram Dass is right when he says part of the problem is that our present-day community has lost touch with nature. If we slow down to take in the beat of the world, we see that every living thing follows a pattern. Dass points out, "The cycles of nature give an intuitive, innate meaning to aging. . . [and] the appropriateness of time and place."[5]

Growing old is not only thoroughly within keeping of the cycles of life, it is utterly *appropriate*. What else are we supposed to do? It would be unnatural for a living entity to remain perpetually young. And the desire for humans in Western society to try to hold back age and pretend youth is forever emergent is a bit absurd.

But absurd we seem to be. Unless we go ahead and buck our crazy system. Unless we decide that our society's dreary view of aging must come to an end.

We shouldn't be pressured into a life stage we left long ago. We need to be where we are in our lives and feel oh so right about it. That's the shift we're after.

What we think,
we become.

Buddha

This is our next task. To think of how we want to be as older people. Then to become what we think.

Most change happens because attitudes change. You can join a progressive aging group, if you like, or write your congress-woman in favor of pro-elder legislation. But the collective whole of our culture is not going to view aging in an enlight-ened way until it does. Experts have provided the ground-work, but we have to *show* each other and the young people around us how we can revolutionize the concept of aging.

How do you let everyone know you've opted for this new paradigm?

1. Stop pretending you're younger than you are or that you want to be younger. It's only making you unhappy. You've already decided you don't want to go back in time. Go ahead and tell people your age. Just stand up and say, I like being (your age here). We demystify the whole aging process when others see we're not afraid of it. That's how you and I become living examples of an elder's majesty.

2. Start throwing the word *old* around more, because there's nothing wrong with those three little letters. We talk about fine old wine or a beautiful old building. Why can't *we* get in on the action? Old rhymes with "bold", and you don't get to be old unless you are.

3. Find ever more words *you* like to describe yourself. Most people don't like *senior*, but I kind of like *advanced human* or just *advanced* as a way to describe us. Some older people are using the term *super adults*, though perhaps that gives too big a nod to adults who already control the conversation. How about *seasoned*? What would you like to call yourself? Try calling yourself that.

4. Be kind to your body. It's been with you from the beginning. Like an old friend, it knows you well, and you know it. Take it to a spa for a massage. Sit it gently in a nice, hot tub for a soak. Treat it to lunch with a friend, and toast how fortunate you and your friend are to have these wonderful, physical selves. Then take your body for a long walk, because you want your beloved to last. Hugs and kisses.

5. Become the eccentric you've always thought was hiding inside. Get your fortune told. Take a cruise on a Great Lakes freighter. Wear your grandmother's jewelry with your ripped jeans—on the freighter. Sport a punk hairdo. Be the new, older you. You're the only one who has to approve.

6. "Be" rather than do. Tell people what you're "being" instead of what you're "doing." If they don't know the

difference, explain the *being* and *doing* concept. If they still don't get it, at least the conversation won't have been all about them.

7. Gently call people on their ageist attitudes. It's part of our elder role. When the guy at the meat counter says, "What can I get for you, young lady?" tell him it's okay with you that you're not a young lady. Say, "I like being an older woman. Aging's a blast, which *you'll* find out in a few years." Smile when you say it, though. Like putting a smiley face at the end of a snarky email, you'll get your point across, and no one's the wiser. ☺

8. Give advice. Tell people that's what elders are for. Young people need the benefit of your experience. They don't have the perspective to know, "This too shall pass" or "Failing isn't as big a deal as you think it is" or "There are plenty of other fish in the sea." Give them examples from your own life to make them feel better. The whole point is to keep younger people from stressing out so much. Then in the end let them figure things out for themselves, because you don't want to be stressed out, either.

9. Live in the moment. Meditate more. Carve out little sections of your day just to take in the world. If someone wants you to do something you don't want to do, remember, you don't have to.

   a. Tell them you can't get together because you're in your Hindu third stage, and you're too busy doing nothing.

b. Let them know you can't meet at a designated time because time doesn't exist. Besides, you and your other you are tied up.

c. Say you're spending time thinking about death, and after you die, you might want to remain in your bedroom for a number of months. If you're lucky, they won't call again.

10. Let younger people know how important it is to be grateful. Tell them the more they show gratitude, the happier they'll be and the longer they'll live. Don't tell them about the weight thing, though, or they won't do it.

11. Nothing speaks louder to the culture than the pocketbook. Be sure to use yours to support products and causes that make you feel better about the older you. That means expensive wrinkle creams are probably out, and weekend trips to the mountains are in. (They cost about the same.) The flashy sports car is out, painting classes and art supplies are in. Constant covering of your gray is out, flowy silver hair is in. Puffy lip injections are out; kissing your true love and enjoying an afternoon of sex is in. I could go on.

Over forty years ago, when Gloria Steinem turned forty, she said, "This is what forty looks like." When she turned fifty, she said, "This is what fifty looks like." I think she has said the same kind of thing almost every decade since. She is trying to get people used to what aging looks like. We have to pull our own Gloria Steinems.

When people think older people look too old to hire, we have to show them what older working people look like.

When society asks what older people contribute, we have to let our knowledge and wisdom speak for itself. And show everyone how elders complete the culture.

When people are busy going from one activity to the next, we have to demonstrate the peace of being in the moment.

When women worry about losing their youthful appearance, we have to show them older beauty in its glory.

When our culture tries to sweep death under the rug, we have to tell people we're not afraid to bring it into the open.

When our young aren't sure how to express themselves, we have to remind them how wonderful it is just to *be* yourself.

When those around us worry about the little things in life, we have to advise them to put life into perspective.

When society tells us, in its many ways, how much it dislikes aging, we have to show society how natural, appropriate, and rewarding aging can be.

We have a big role here. If a shift in cultural attitudes is to take place, we need to let everyone know how all of society will benefit. Mostly we need to clue ourselves in. We have to take a risk, like the risks we took when we were the young generation. We need to let go of the side of the pool and swim on our own.

As William Thomas argues, when elderhood becomes a valued part of our culture, the other stages of the life cycle become more distinct and valuable too. Maybe our society will be less about moving kids into adulthood too quickly (and trying to keep elders as perpetual "adults") and more about honoring each life stage.

"Aging is the most human thing we do,"[6] says Thomas in *What Are Old People For?* The later stage of life allows us to do what other sentient beings never can: reflect, advise, harvest our experience, perspective and wisdom, and even transcend.

As elders we show others what being human looks like.

❮**Craft** *your own version of a paradigm shift.*
How would you like to blossom as you age?
How can our culture help you do that?❯

Who is the real you? What qualities do you think are the essence of who you are?

How can you allow more of the real you to bloom in your everyday life?

What one or two steps could you take to begin your transition into the elder (the real you) you'd like to be?

What is holding you back? If you're reluctant to let go of "adulthood" and embrace your later years (i.e. "elderhood" or whatever you like calling it), what are you worried about losing?

What could you gain from moving into your new, elder stage?

Describe an older person you admire. What is in his or her nature that you find most appealing?

How has age enhanced his/her best qualities?

If someone were to say he or she admired you, which of your qualities do you think that person would find inspiring?

Fantasize about a paradigm shift. How different would our culture look if elders took their rightful place in the life cycle?

How do you imagine the culture supporting your own unfolding as an elder?

Is it okay for older people to ask for respect from others in our society? How would we go about doing it?

How would you like your own children to view their later years?

Can you be their "elder" role model?

If our society could make one change today that would help you feel better about growing older, what would it be?

How can you start to bring about this change yourself?

"The dogs bark, but the caravan moves on," a thoughtful colleague once said to me. Change will happen. There will be resistance, but humankind ultimately moves forward. What will "forward" look like for us? What will it look like for you?

The more important question is the second one, because without each of you making your own shift in attitude about aging, there won't be any entity known as change. You're the one who has to buck the system and create your own significant old age. Thanks in advance for making the next chapter possible.

Chapter Seventeen
What Are You Doing the Rest of Your Life?

Mbah Gotho, who lives in Idonesia, is 149. He was born in 1870 and says he has documentation to prove it.[1] That means when Mr. Gotho was my age, he wasn't even halfway through life. What if he'd had to figure out, back then, what to do with the rest of his years?

Do human beings live this long? People who keep tabs on these sorts of things are trying to verify the age of the venerable Mr. Gotho, but even if he's only 110, he's still lived a remarkable amount of time.

Some scientists think it *is* possible for people to live into their 140s and beyond. David Sinclair of the Harvard Medical School believes we can eventually reverse some of the physical markers of aging. It won't be too far-fetched, he claims, to see humans with a lifespan of a century and a half in the not-too-distant future.[2] Sinclair then adds that someone who may live that long has probably already been born. Yes. It's Mr. Gotho.

But Dr. Sinclair is talking about children today whose longevity could be extraordinary. Maybe your grandchildren will last well into their hundreds. It's hard to predict how different life could be for those long-lived people. Will their view of growing older change radically? Will the whole concept of elderhood as we know it become less important?

I think it will become *more* important. With a life cycle that includes a longer adulthood and a lengthy old age, there may be more emphasis on figuring out what we are going to be during all these years.

Imagine the possibilities. Young people will have time to consider their options and learn about themselves. They may even slow down enough to reflect on the world around them. Adults, with less pressure to build a career quickly, will have room to try a variety of work options. Risk and mistakes can be part of career exploration, and success may take on more personal meaning.

Come to think of it, that new way of living has many of the hallmarks of "elderhood;" pacing yourself, being yourself, enjoying the moment, and exploring possibilities that appeal to you. By living longer we may extend some of the balance of an elder life to all age groups. It can happen when constraints are loosened and the stress of time lifted. Life could be that way for people who expect to live as long as Mr. Gotho.

The practical among you no doubt wonder how all these old, really old people are going to support themselves in their very late years. That noteworthy concern is the reason society will have to take on the century-and-a-half life cycle with lots of creativity. We will be forced to look at all life stages in new ways, particularly old age.

In a world with prolonged human life, experience and wisdom—the kinds that set older people apart—become the treasured commodities they were meant to be. We will use the guidance of elders in schools, in government, on community projects, in city planning, in conserving our resources, and in building one-to-one relationships with people in other parts of the world. The ancient role of the elder *is* the means by which elders will live and find fulfillment.

But what if you, as an elder with super-life expectancy, don't want to spend your days sharing your wisdom with others?

You may think you don't want to, but trust me, you do. For one thing, offering your wisdom, understanding, and compassion to those around you comes naturally with age. And the act of giving yourself away, which is what you do when you spread your wisdom around, is almost a sure path to happiness.

> *If you want others to be happy, practice compassion.*
> *If you want to be happy, practice compassion.*
>
> Dalai Lama

By giving of yourself in a compassionate way, you activate neurotransmitters in the brain that bring on "feelings of reward." What's more, these "feel-good chemicals" can be addictive,[3] which means you may end up volunteering wisdom right and left in spite of yourself.

Looking at our lives from the long view, happiness has to figure into it mightily. Happiness is the absolute basis for being kind to our aging selves. It is the whole point of asserting our right to grow old. Giving away our wisdom, even if we only do it occasionally, is one element of a happy life. Learning to abide change, almost at the other end of the spectrum, is another.

As we grow older, change can be disconcerting. Sometimes we feel out of touch with what's going on. Young people talk a language we don't understand and do things we never thought of doing. Drones fly by our windows, and robots mow the neighbor's yard. The world feels a little foreign. Are we still part of it?

We are. Not part of the young herd, as we used to be, but we are the ones to bring steadiness to what can seem like strange territory. By being here we help everyone else put existence into perspective. And from the length of time we've lived, we know change is at the core of things.

> *Change is never painful,*
> *only resistance to change is painful.*
>
>   Buddha

Understanding impermanence is the essence of Buddhist teaching. Buddhists will tell you nothing in the universe remains the same, even moment to moment. That's why it's important to reside *in* the moment, because according to believers, it's all we have.

Even when the moment is unpleasant, it helps to understand that it's only a moment. We don't know what the next one will bring. Being right here, right now means we're not imagining a future with yet gloomier prospects. The future will be made up of moments too, each new, each as impermanent as present moments are now.

When we meditate, thoughts can float through our minds. What we try to do is look at them without judgment, set them to the side if we wish, and come back to our breathing. The thoughts we have while meditating are not unlike change as we often experience it. Change also comes upon us, and we observe it. We can let it drift by us or engage it and delight in it. We don't have to fight change; we don't even have to react to it. But we do have to appreciate its inevitability.

Matthieu Ricard is content with change. At sixty-nine he's content with almost everything. Ricard, a Buddhist monk who lives in Nepal, is known as the happiest man in the world. How did he manage that?

Remember the scientists back in chapter eight who measured gamma waves of monks' brains? They found that Buddhist monks who meditated religiously had more activity in the part of the brain that controls positive emotions. Well, Ricard, one of the monks, was apparently off the chart in gamma waves, so much so that scientists started calling him "the world's happiest man."[4]

If we want to be happier as we age, we can only hope a bit of Ricard's good cheer rubs off on us. What does he know that we don't? For one thing, he says happiness can be learned. It's simply a matter of acquiring a few skills: "benevolence, attention, emotional balance, and resilience."[5]

Do these characteristics sound like skills? To me they're more like attributes. Maybe much like the attributes of an elder. That is, the giving of yourself with compassion, paying attention to what's around you (being in the moment), keeping your emotional state in balance, and maintaining resilience.

You could say these "skills" come along with age. But it seems we have to cultivate our strengths if we want them to be a steadfast influence in our lives. According to Ricard, we have to *practice* benevolence, attention, emotional balance, and resilience.

You've probably heard the adage, "Fake it till you make it." I think that's what he's talking about. See yourself as a kind, attentive, balanced, and flexible human being. Fake it at first if you must, and you will improve your chances of becoming precisely that person.

You could even try this fake-it-till-you-make-it thing as an experiment. Let the higher you (the thoughtful and balanced you) make the decisions. Step back and give yourself room to be objective. It's only an experiment. Try it and see if it works. Ask yourself, what would Ricard do?

One more piece of "happiest man" advice: spend fifteen minutes a day thinking positive thoughts. Set aside a little time. Bend your brain into a lighthearted state. Let positive currents flow. Here's why you need to do it, according to Ricard: "Typically when we experience feelings of happiness and love, it's fleeting, and then something else happens, and we move on to the next thought." He says we don't always take time to let the good moments sink in.[6] We need to have at least fifteen minutes of happy thought waves bouncing through our heads every day.

Looking for happiness is looking no further than ourselves. We've heard this all our lives. The ability to be happy is inside. We only need to coax it out. I think the act of coaxing is easier when we're in love. And not necessarily with another person. We're happiest when we're in love with ourselves.

Does this idea take narcissism to a new level?

Not in the least. Being in love with the person you are means you accept all that makes you human. You believe in yourself despite the kinks. You know how to care for and nurture you, and you look out for your own well-being. I hope by this time in your life you are thoroughly in love with who you are, not that you can't change a few habits or get along better with a prickly brother-in-law.

But the essence of you should not be in question. You cannot give of yourself completely, be content in the moment, embrace aging, work out differences with an off-putting relative, or feel truly happy unless you trust in your own value.

The love of you, your value, is the basis for making happiness your centerpiece going forward. Speaking of what's ahead, do you have a bucket list?

We're all supposed to have one. You know, a list of things that will make you happy before you, like Jimmy Durante in the movie *It's a Mad, Mad, Mad, Mad World,* send a bucket flying. I ran into a friend at the grocery the other day who just got back from a cruise through Vietnam. "Is it on your bucket list?" he asked. "Life changing!"

I can't get into traditional bucket lists, perhaps because they are often a catalog of marvelous places to visit or things to do that we can't wait to cross off so we can get on to the next one. A cynical take, I know. But to me a bucket list hints of one-upping friends and acquaintances whose ambitions may not be as creative or taxing as ours. Once again we're competing. We're *doing.* We're not *being.*

New York Times columnist David Brooks, who wrote *The Road to Character,* references "a moral bucket list" in a *Times* essay adapted from his book. In it he says, if you "live for external achievement, years pass and the deepest parts of you go unexplored and unstructured."[7]

"External achievement" sounds like an item on a run-of-the-mill bucket list.

Brooks is talking about something more profound: a list of actions we can take if we want to give of ourselves. A list that will bring the joy of flowing gamma waves. As he sees it, our "list" should not be about "being better than others," but about "being better" people.[8] It's a noble and happiness-inducing thought.

I also like the idea of a list that includes reconnecting with old friends or patching up a strained relationship in your family. Or you could always throw yourself a seventieth birthday fling surrounded by everyone you love. These aren't ambitions requiring lots of money or free time, but they may end up being more enriching than those that do.

Let's put together our own list. On it we should record pursuits that will make us happy. Use the "eat dessert first" rule. The idea is to put stuff at the top of the list that would bring you real contentment. Go for these, the whipped cream and chocolate cake.

1. What's your favorite daydream?

2. Could this daydream be translated into some kind of reality for you? Are there things you dream about that you would like to pursue? Could even an aspect of some of these favorite thoughts be integrated into your daily life?

3. What endeavors, travel destinations, old or new relationships would bring you the most happiness? How could you make some of these long-held desires happen?

4. Who would you like to reconnect with from your past?

5. What's keeping you from reconnecting?

6. If you could mend a few fences, where would you like to start? What relationship (with a friend, relative, or even casual acquaintance) do you want to improve?

7. What's the one thing you could do to be a better person, as David Brooks suggests? The point is to make yourself happy. It's about having more benevolence or emotional balance in your life, much to the approval of Matthieu Ricard. How would you become that better, happier person now?

What if everyone in the world did this? Think about it for a second. What if everyone in the world decided to do one thing that would help him or her be a better person? Then each of us practiced that one thing and made it a part of us. What if we all came slightly more into emotional balance?

There would probably be a subtle shift in the world as we know it. It might be barely discernable, but it would be there—a small and pleasant change of course in human interactions. We would feel it, in ourselves and in each other.

Not everyone has the maturity or wherewithal to make even small changes. But elders have this potential. It's part of the province of an elder: the perspective to see what needs to be done and the maturity to follow through on it, if we so desire. As we age there's often an unbridled sense of "why not?" What's to stop us from what we want or who we need to be?

We can make a shift in how we relate to people in our lives. We can alter what we're engaged in, day to day, to make ourselves happier. We have influenced the world. Now we can use that influence on ourselves, which, in its way, will again affect everyone else.

Jonas Salk once asked, looking at the long view, are we being good ancestors?[9] If we're being good to ourselves, we are building the base for future generations to construct their own notable old age. What we think about ourselves, how we tend to ourselves and encourage each other in our later years, will not only affect how others treat us now, but it will make old age a better place for those who follow.

Are we exaggerating, then, when we say your happiness is important, not only to you but to many other people? I don't think so.

The beauty of the human life cycle is that each separate stage of it affects every other part. Happier elders will help adults see that later years are not a sad ride on the downslope. Adults may even be enticed to look forward to elderhood, tossing aside their darkest views of old age.

Children can also sense a change in how we feel about ourselves. They may find greater security in their own exploratory time of life, seeing that even the elder stage has importance and rewards. With elderhood better defined, each person can feel more content with his or her place in the continuum.

We are older now. Open, curious, wise, self-reflective, spiritual, confident, balanced, gentle, present, grateful, and with a knowing about time and death that the younger may not be privy to. We don't want to be superficial. We can't pretend anymore. We are elders, and we're in love with our older selves.

It's good, then, that we go ahead and take one more step to complete our own projection of an elder future. It involves creating a specific mental picture of who we want to be.

Here's mine:

I am looking out at the ocean. All the way to the horizon I see peaks of waves, millions of them, bobbing together, blinking with sunlight. Closer in, waves roll onto the beach, slide back, and come forward again with luxurious monotony.

The sand is warm. I'm sitting on a chair barefoot in some sort of grass or bamboo beach hut, sheltered on three sides but open to the water. In front of me is a desk anchored in the sand with my laptop on it, and I'm writing, writing all day with a breeze in my face. I have a sketch pad with me because I may want to draw, though I'm not good at it. I also have a fancy camera I can pick up anytime I want to.

I take time for a little lunch, read a book, walk along the flat, wet sand. Then I'm back in my beach shelter, facing the waves. I'm wearing bunches of leather bracelets, a faded T-shirt, and a sarong. I have on my gold earrings from Portugal as I type away before the sun goes down.

This is how I see myself as an elder. It's my fantasy of how I would like to spend my days. If happiness and the celebration of life's most important stage are my touchstones going forward, I have to keep this idyll front and center in my mind. If I can imagine a perfect version of my older self, I may be able to make pieces of my daydream come true.

You probably think my thinking is a little crazy. Who sits on a beach all day? Isn't this fairy tale just that, something that can never come to pass?

To which I would say, this incarnation of an elder, reclaiming her right to grow old, is an *ideal*. It's make-believe. But what I want is to come as close as possible to this projection of myself, however it may manifest. Because the thought of living unencumbered on a beach makes me happy.

Let's take the crazy out of it. What *can* I do to bring what I see in my head into my life? I can spend more time writing. I can continue to sketch things, even though the stuff I draw isn't all that great. I can use my camera more and take beach vacations when I can afford them. I can dress in a less structured way. Go barefoot. All things are possible.

Having a picture in your mind of what makes you happy is

essential. The more you can see a relaxed and engaged you, the more likely "this you" will reveal itself. What are you doing the rest of your life? It's your turn.

❰See *yourself in your own, ideal elder image.* ❱

Envision feeling content, at peace, happy. Where are you? What are you involved in? Who is with you? Are you inside or outdoors? What are you wearing? Form a clear snapshot in your mind.

Bring this image with you as you write out a couple of paragraphs describing your most enchanting elder self.

I am after an effortless, boundary-less way to live. I want to feel as timeless as I can and present to moments that are happening now. Do you feel this way?

Our reward for the years we have lived is to follow our desires going forward. This means keeping our elder image continually in our heads and checking ourselves often: Am I leaning toward things that contribute to this ideal depiction of me? Am I leaning away from circumstances and actions that don't? Most of all, am I living a life that makes me happy, that is my right as an older person?

I hope that, even a little bit, Mr. Gotho is. Because all the signs tell us this is how we were meant to grow old.

OUTTAKES

Stuff that didn't make the author's cut, so it ended up here.

1. Women don't live longer than men. It just seems longer.

   Kathleen O.

2. Whether you plan to live a long life or a super-long one that breaks records, it never hurts to find out more about yourself. Have you thought of mapping your own ancestry by having your DNA analyzed? A lot of companies will do it for you, and it's fun to find out what you're made of. I sent off swabs of my DNA and found out I was more than 42% Scandinavian. And 16% Italian. I had no idea. What a gift to finally figure out why I like Norwegian authors and spaghetti.

3. A friend told me she has started making regular appointments with herself. Her purpose is to zero in on what will make her happier. She takes a pen, and a notepad and goes to a coffee shop alone. I love this idea. Put yourself on your calendar (who's more important than you?), sit down in some nice surroundings, and give serious thought to your own joy. What day are you free? Buy yourself a latte.

4. "Laughter is a good natural tranquilizer," says Dr. Raymond Moody author of *Laugh After Laugh: The Healing Power of Humor.*[1] "It can stimulate the brain to. . .trigger the release of endorphins." You know, the body's natural opiate, which is legal in every state. There's even such a thing as "laughter yoga," and it's almost better than wine. You can follow it up with a real glass after class.

5. It turns out the Dalai Lama laughs a lot. I have this on excellent authority from a woman who has spent time with him. Margaret Cruikshank, author of *Learning to be Old*, concurs: "The Dalai Lama's playful spirit is one of his most engaging characteristics."[2] Does his playfulness make him laugh? Or does his laughter make him playful? Both.

6. There was a full-page ad in our local paper recently for a national chain of independent assisted living and memory-care facilities. An employee of the chain was quoted in the ad saying, "Stop treating seniors like old people!" I thought, but we *are* old people, and there's nothing wrong with being old. Surely a for-profit organization that purports to serve "seniors" should be in the forefront of dispelling aging stereotypes. Treat us like old people, please. Give us priority boarding on aircraft, and when we're not traveling, show us respect and affection, because we've earned both.

7. I have a younger friend who is married to an older man. I've known her for years, but she's never told me her husband's age. "You know Dan doesn't like to talk about age," she said. As he approached a benchmark birthday this year, she told me, "Dan is going to be eighty, but please keep this confidential." I did. I changed the circumstances and name of this person so I could include it in this book. But I still feel bad. Because Dan is ashamed of turning eighty. At this point in his life he should feel at ease with his age, enjoying a sense of accomplishment for having reached a significant milestone. Don't make Dan's mistake.

8. Speaking of old, for decades gerontologists have divided the aging population into four groups: Prime of life generation (ages fifty to sixty-four), Young-old (sixty-five to seventy-four), Old-old (seventy-five to eighty-four), and Oldest-old (eighty-five plus). Are these designations outmoded? Do we need a category for the Super-old? Or should we do away with categories altogether? Older people should have a say in this.

9. The study of gerontology as a science didn't begin until after World War II, maybe because there weren't enough people living long enough to warrant a whole area of research. Now that there are so many of us, right up through the "super-old," we're going to need a bigger effort with a lot more professionals to help us navigate this exceptional life stage.

10. We have lost some of the beauty of elders passing along their stories to future generations. We don't sit around communal fires in the evening anymore and offer our wisdom to the younger around us. In *What Are Old People For?*, William Thomas argues that ancient storytelling has been replaced by modern technology— the Internet, TV, and movies. These technologies often tell a different tale about who we are than our elders would.[3] Are we losing some continuity in our cultural heritage by not encouraging elder storytelling? It's never too late to start your own tradition.

11. It's interesting what people remember about us. We go out in the world and interact with friends and strangers but don't often think about how we influence others. Have you ever had an old friend recount an experience you had together, something you're somewhat vague on, and yet he remembers the whole thing? Then he tells you how much the experience meant to him? Multiply that by hundreds of times, and you begin to get an idea of the impact your life is having on others. It's comforting to think about how much each of us has contributed to the human narrative. And if your story is passed along to yet another person, how lasting your influence can be.

12. Ram Dass, about our relationship to others, wrote in the introduction to his book, *Polishing the Mirror:*

> I honor the place in you
> Where if you are in that place in you and

I am in that place in me,
There is only one of us.

Namaste.[4]

> Ram Dass
> Maui
> August 2013

13. What is the purpose of life? At age eighty-five Florida Scott Maxwell wrote this: "Our whole duty may be to clarify and increase what we are, to make our consciousness a finer quality."[5] These words are in the final few sentences of Thomas Cole's influential book, *The Journey of Life.*

14. Regarding death, *The Tibetan Book of Living and Dying* says:

> *Perhaps the deepest reason why we are afraid of death is because we do not know who we are.*[6]

This is why we need to follow Florida Scott Maxwell's advice: make "our consciousness a finer quality." That means, in part, becoming more aware of who we are. Just as Socrates advised us to know ourselves. I might add, we should also get comfortable with our own spirituality. This is part of knowing too. It can provide consolation for the unknowable, which goes to the heart of death.

15. While we're chatting about death, have you written your obituary yet? I wrote mine as an exercise for a class I was teaching several years ago. I included some personal observations and mentioned a few idiosyncrasies. I like reading obits, and I particularly like ones that are humorous or give insight into the kind of person the departed was. I often wonder if the good ones were written by the person himself. When you write your own, you have some control over how you want people to remember you. You can make your death notice fun or offbeat. And you save those left behind from the sad chore of having to write yours. Precisely why more obits aren't good for a laugh.

16. Did you know thinking about death can make you funny? Turns out, several years ago, two researchers found that participants in a study who were "subliminally primed" to concentrate on death or pain wrote funnier captions to cartoons than those who weren't[7]. Think of the implications here. You could ruminate about death so much that you finish your fourth Hindu stage doing stand-up.

17. Finally, have you ever noticed that people who say, "long story short" have already told you a long story? You've heard mine. Here's the short version:

> You're supposed to grow old.
> You're supposed to be happy.

You'd think both would be obvious, but I had to write a whole book about it.

Postscript

This past year I turned seventy and found my patience waning. First, my cat died. Ten days later my dear mother-in-law, Dorothy, passed away. A month after that, my ex-husband was diagnosed with Alzheimer's disease.

Each of these events has been stressful in its own way. I have grieved, and I have thought a lot about the end of life, theirs and my own. Yes, it's a downer to think about death all the time, but as I have pointed out, seventy is not fifty. With seventy comes the realization that I, like my cat, will die. The difference between her and me is that I know I am going to go.

This explains some of my impatience. I don't have years to fool around. I can't indulge people who want me to do endless things for them—from telemarketers with their phone pitch (stop interrupting me, I am not going to buy anything from you) to other people who want something from me.

Even family. Oh, I'm nice enough to them; I love them. But I've been setting a lot more boundaries of late. My life ahead seems short compared to the anticipated future of some of my family members. And like most women, I've already spent years trying to make family and friends happy. It's their turn to defer to me.

I admit I'm also a little annoyed by all of this. I should've set more limits years ago. I should've put myself first more often. I should've spoken up. But better late than never.

I'm starting to take on the role of a curmudgeon. And I can see why younger people think older people are cranky. You would be too, if your days were winding down.

Another thought has occurred to me. Maybe my personality is evolving this way because I'm out of estrogen. I am finally catching up with men, the estrogen-bereft, who have always been comfortable speaking up and haven't had to worry about making everybody feel good.

Most men I've encountered in my professional life have felt it well within their rights to be blunt, to cut the chit chat and say what's on their minds. I don't think in the whole of my career I've ever been called blunt.

So, I'm trying out a new persona, lit by a desire not to waste moments. Armed with less estrogen and the slow fade in front of me, I am impatiently living life in my seventies.

I'm not sure how I feel about it yet. I don't know that I've completely come to terms with being in my eighth decade and losing those who are close to me in quick succession.

I've learned that growing old is both limiting and liberating. It's liberating, in part, because it is limited. My mother-in-law undoubtedly knew this. My ex-husband may have some inkling of this even as his appreciation of the world slips away.

I'm leaning heavily on being liberated. I can see how this quality can expand in me as I age. It's a gift from the human cycle of life as I grow old and become more aware of the truth of things. My dear cat didn't know what she was missing.

End Notes

Chapter 2

1. Deepak Singh, "A Ga. School Bans the Greeting 'Namaste'. Do They Know What it Means?," Goats and Soda on npr.org, July 26, 2015, accessed August 2020, https://www.npr.org/sections/goatsandsoda/2015/07/26/425968146/whats-in-a-namaste-depends-if-you-live-in-india-or-the-u-s

2. LiPo, as quoted by Jon Kabat-Zinn, *Wherever You Go, There You Are* (New York: Hyperion, 1994), 140.

3. Mwalimu Imarra, as quoted by Mark Nepo, *The Book of the Awakening* (San Francisco: Conari Press, 2011), 31.

4. Jean Baudrillard, as quoted by Robert Kastenbaum, *The Psychology of Death,* 3rd ed. (New York: Springer, 2000), 99.

5. Thomas R. Cole, *The Journey of Life* (New York: Cambridge University Press, 1992), 110.

6. Ibid.

7. Health Inequality Project, 2019, accessed July, 2020, http://healthinequality.org

8. William H. Thomas, *What Are Old People For?* (St. Louis: VanderWyk & Burnham, 2004), 82.

9. Ibid., 15.

10. Ibid., 16.

11. Cole, *The Journey of Life*, 116.

12. Robert N. Butler, *Why Survive? Being Old in America* (Baltimore: Johns Hopkins University Press, 1975), 1.

13. Thomas Moore, Care of the Soul: Joyfully Adrift, October 21, 2013, accessed July, 2020, https://spiritualityhealth. com/articles/2013/10/21/care-soul-joyfully-adrift

CHAPTER 3

1. William Graham Sumner, as quoted by Butler, *Why Survive?*, 19.

2. Thomas R. Cole, Sally A Gadow, eds., *What Does It Mean to Grow Old?* (Durham: Duke University Press, 1986), 3.

3. Ruth Snowdon, *Teach Yourself Jung* (London: Hodder Education, 2006), 78.

4. Joseph Campbell, ed., *The Portable Jung* (New York: Viking Penguin Inc., 1971), 17.

5. Erik Erikson, as quoted by Cole, *The Journey of Life*, xix.

6. Dr. David B. Reuben, as quoted by Douglas Martin, obituary for Robert Butler, *New York Times*, July 7, 2010, National edition.

7. Martin, quoting Robert Butler, obituary for Robert Butler, *New York Times*.

8. Butler, quoting Maggie Kuhn, *Why Survive?*, 341.

9. Ibid.

10. Robert N. Butler, *The Longevity Revolution* (New York: Perseus Books Group, 2008), 4.

11. Ibid.
12. Kate Zernite, "Turn 70. Act Your Grandchild's Age." *New York Times*, July 10, 2010, National edition.
13. Ibid.
14. Ibid.
15. Harry Moody, "The Meaning of Life and Old Age" in *What Does It Mean to Grow Old?*, eds. Cole and Gadow, 22.
16. Ibid., 12.
17. Harry Moody, "Conscious Aging: A New Level of Growth in Later Life," 2002, accessed September, 2020, http://www.wellnessgoods.com/consciousaging newlevel.asp
18. Thomas, *What Are Old People For?*, 133-135.
19. Ibid., 132.
20. Ibid.
21. Ibid., 124.
22. Lewis Richmond, *Aging as a Spiritual Practice* (New York: Gotham Books, 2012), 206.

CHAPTER 4

1. HH The Dalai Lama and Howard C. Cutler, M.D., *The Art of Happiness* (New York: Riverhead Books, 1998), 18.
2. Carl Jung as quoted by Campbell, ed., *The Portable Jung*, 17.
3. Robert C. Atchley, "Living From the Light," in *The Inner Work of Eldering*, 2nd ed., eds. Bolton Anthony, Ron Pevny, and Judith Helburn (Chapel Hill, NC: Second Journey Publications, 2011), 2.

4. Ram Dass, *Still Here* (New York: The Berkley Publishing Group, 2000), 24.

5. Sogyal Rinpoche, *The Tibetan Book of Living and Dying* (New York: HarperOne, 2002), 35-36.

CHAPTER 5

1. Thomas, *What Are Old People For?*, 116.

2. Ibid., 117.

3. Ibid., 118.

4. Ibid.

5. M.C. Richards, *Centering in Pottery, Poetry, and the Person*, 2nd ed. (Middletown, Connecticut: Wesleyan University Press, 1989), 135.

6. Mihaly Csikszentmihalyi, *Flow* (New York: Harper Perennial Modern Classics, 2008), 4.

7. Ibid., 6.

8. Ibid.

9. Thich Nhat Hanh, *Peace Is Every Step* (New York: Bantam Books, 1992), 40.

CHAPTER 6

1. Emily Yeh, *Taming Tibet: Landscape Transformation and the Gift of Chinese Development* (Ithaca, NY: Cornell University Press, 2013), introduction.

2. Ibid.

3. Dan Allender, *Sabbath* (Nashville, Tennessee: Thomas Nelson, 2009), 4.

4. Ibid., 47.

5. Tilden Edwards, *Sabbath Time* (Nashville: Upper

Room Books, 1992), 52.

6. Ibid., 54.
7. Mark Bittman, "I Need a Virtual Break. No, Really.," *New York Times*, March 2, 2008, National edition.
8. Allender, *Sabbath*, 15.
9. Paul Salopek, "A Stroll Around the World," *New York Times*, November 22, 2013, National edition.
10. Marcy Heidish, *Soul and the City* (Colorado Springs, CO: Waterbrook Press, 2008), 79-80.
11. Ibid., 78.
12. Allender, *Sabbath*, 165.
13. Edwards, *Sabbath Time*, 99.
14. Dan Buettner, "The Island Where People Forget to Die," *New York Times*, October 24, 2012, National edition.
15. Dass, *Still Here*, 145.
16. Ibid., 202.

CHAPTER 7

1. Thomas, *What Are Old People For?*, 11.
2. Deepak Chopra, *Reinventing the Body, Resurrecting the Soul*, (New York: Three Rivers Press, 2009), 248.
3. Ibid., 249.
4. Moore, Care of the Soul: Joyfully Adrift, October 21, 2013, accessed July, 2020, https://spiritualityhealth.com/articles/2013/10/21/care-soul-joyfully-adrift
5. Butler, *The Longevity Revolution*, 14.
6. Louise Aronson as quoted by Joseph Epstein, "The Way We Age Now," *Wall Street Journal*, January 18-19, 2020, National edition.

7. Bernard Mambo as quoted by Thomas, *What Are Old People For?*, 59.
8. Ibid.

CHAPTER 8

1. Zen Master Seung Sahn, *Zen, The Perfect Companion* (New York: Black Dog & Levanthal Publishers, 2003), 15.
2. Kabat-Zinn, *Wherever You Go, There You Are*, 96.
3. Frank M. Wanderer, PhD, quotes Carl Jung, November 8, 2016, accessed August, 2020, https://themindunleashed.com/?s=Frank+M.+Wanderer%2C+Jung
4. Chopra, *Reinventing the Body, Resurrecting the Soul*, 246.
5. Butler, *Why Survive?*, 412.
6. Ibid., 413.
7. Jon Batiste as quoted by Howie Kahn, "Jon Batiste on Music and His New Gig on the 'Late Show'," *WSJ Magazine*, September 8, 2015, National edition.
8. Ron Pevney, The Inner Work of Conscious Eldering, accessed August, 2020, https://www.centerforconsciouseldering.com/2017/04/13/the-inner-work-of-conscious-eldering/
9. His Holiness the Dalai Lama, Howard C. Cutler, MD, *The Art of Happiness*, (New York: Riverhead Books, 1998), 43.
10. Ibid., 63.
11. "Understanding the Johari Window Model" on selfawareness.org.uk, November 10, 2013, accessed August 2020, https://www.selfawareness.org.uk/news/

understanding-the-johari-window-model
12. Tenzin Wangyal Rinpoche as quoted by Nick Polizzi, Stillness, Silence, Spaciousness, January 23, 2014, accessed August, 2020, https://www.thesacredscience. com/stillness-silence-spaciousness/
13. Dass, *Still Here*, 115.
14. Tibetan Buddhist saying as quoted by Dass, Ibid., 114.
15. Adiba Osmani, The Link Between Happiness and Meditation, 2013, accessed August, 2020, https://bi-dushi.com/link-happiness-meditation/
16. Dr. Ronald Siegel, What is the connection between mindfulness and happiness?, 2015, accessed August, 2020, https://www.sharecare.com/health/meditation/what-connection-between-mindfulness-happiness
17. Jon Kabat-Zinn, "Mindfulness Meditation: Health Benefits of An Ancient Buddhist Practice," Daniel Goleman and Joel Gurin, eds., *Mind, Body Medicine: How to Use Your Mind for Better Health* (Yonkers, NY: Consumer Reports Books, 1993), 271.
18. Giovanni Dienstmann, 7 Tips to Experience Deep Meditation, September, 2015, accessed August, 2020, https://liveanddare.com/deep-meditation/?r_done=1
19. Isabel Allende, "A Beautiful Mind," *Porter*, Winter Escape, 2015, Issue 12, 79.

Chapter 9

1. Cole, *The Journey of Life*, 67.
2. Ibid.
3. Ibid., 69.
4. Csikszentmihalyi, *Flow*, 74.

5. Kabat-Zinn, *Wherever You Go, There You Are*, 53.
6. Seng-Ts'an as quoted by Nepo, *The Book of the Awakening* , 68.

CHAPTER 10

1. Henry Wadsworth Longfellow as quoted by Dass, *Still Here*, 79.
2. Thomas Brinton, Bishop of Rochester, England, as quoted by Cole, *The Journey of Life*, 6.
3. Philosophy 312: Oriental Philosophy; Hinduism: The Four Stages of Life on *p.l.e*, October 28, 2000, accessed August, 2020, https://philosophy.lander.edu/oriental/stages.html
4. Ibid.
5. NAP 411, Spirituality and Aging, Louis Harris and Associates poll (NCOA 2002), 2009, accessed August, 2020, https://www.nap411.com/family/spirituality-a-aging/spirituality-a-aging
6. Thomas, *What Are Old People For?*, 27.
7. Ibid., 27-29.
8. Polly Francis, as quoted by Zalman Schachter-Shalomi, Robert S. Miller, *From Age-ing to Sage-ing* (New York: Hachette Book Group, 1997), 150.
9. Thomas, *What Are Old People For?*, 29.
10. Dass, *Still Here*, 30.
11. Gerard W. Hughes SJ, "Is There a Spirituality for the Elderly?" in *Spirituality and Ageing*, ed. Albert Jewel (Philadelphia: Jessica Kingsley Publishers, 1999), 19.
12. Jack Kornfield, ed., *Teachings of The Buddha* (Boston: Shambhala Publications, Inc., 1993), ix.

13. Ibid.

14. Timber Hawkeye, "Faithfully Religionless," *Science of Mind: Guide for Spiritual Living*, January 2016, 15.

15. Thomas Moore, *A Religion of One's Own* (New York: Gotham Books, 2015), 253.

16. Ibid., 270.

17. Csikszentmihalyi, *Flow*, 76.

18. Ralph Waldo Emerson as quoted by Moore, *A Religion of One's Own*, 271.

19. Eckhart Tolle, *A New Earth* (New York: Plume, 2006), 207.

20. Moore, *A Religion of One's Own*, 270.

CHAPTER 11

1. Carl Jung as quoted by Campbell, ed., *The Portable Jung*, 18.

2. Ibid.

3. The Buddha as quoted by Nepo, *The Book of the Awakening*, 225.

4. Margaret Cruikshank, *Learning to Be Old* (Lanham, Maryland: Rowman & Littlefield Publishers, Inc., 2009), 9.

5. Schachter-Shalomi and Miller, *From Ageing to Sageing*, 145.

6. Thomas, *What Are Old People For?*, 291.

7. Schachter-Shalomi and Miller, *From Ageing to Sageing*, 145.

8. Stephen S. Hall, "Wisdom, Long a Subject for Philosophers, Is Now Being Scrutinized by a Cadre of Scientific Researchers . .," *New York Times Magazine*,

May 6, 2007.

9. Ibid.

10. Ibid.

11. Ibid.

12. Ibid.

13. Phyllis Korkki, "The Science of Older and Wiser," *New York Times*, March 12, 2014, accessed August 2020, https://www.nytimes.com/2014/03/13/business/retirementspecial/the-science-of-older-and-wiser.html

14. Ibid.

15. Ibid.

16. Thomas, *What Are Old People For?*, 57.

17. Angeles Arrien, Ph.D., *The Second Half of Life* (Boulder, Colorado: Sounds True, Inc., 2007), 17.

18. Rabbi Yitzchak Ginsberg as quoted by David Sanders, "The Core of Awareness—Holding Opposites," Kabbalah Experience class, September, 2016, 9.

19. Ibid., 10.

20. Lao Tsu as quoted by David Sanders, Ibid., 11.

CHAPTER 12

1. Marcy Heidish, " Changing Skin" in *Where Do Things Go?* (Colorado Springs, CO: D & A Publisher, 2015), 8.

2. Thomas, *What Are Old People For?*, 23.

3. Bobbi Emel, "How Do the Elderly Become More Resilient?" on Med Page Today, 3/8/12, accessed August, 2020, https://www.kevinmd.com/blog/2012/03/elderly-resilient.html

4. Ibid.

5. Thomas, *What Are Old People For?*, 23-24 .

6. Ibid., 24.

7. Joe Coscarelli, "'The World's Forever Changing,'" *New York Times*, July 19, 2015, National edition.

8. Megan Gannon, "Optimism is the Key to Successful Aging" on livescience.com, December 7, 2012, accessed July, 2020, https://www.livescience.com/25327-optimism-successful-aging.html

9. Dr. Andrew Weil, *Healthy Aging* (New York: Alfred A. Knopf, 2005), 115.

10. Ibid., 214.

11. Michael Puett, Christine Gross-Loh, "The College of Chinese Wisdom," *Wall Street Journal*, April 2-3, 2016, National edition.

CHAPTER 13

1. Ann E. Schlosser, "The Sweet Taste of Gratitude: Feeling Grateful Increases Choice and Consumption of Sweets," *Journal of Consumer Psychology* 25, no.4 (October 2015) : 561-576.

2. Philip C. Watkins, *Gratitude and the Good Life* (New York: Springer Dordrecht Heidelberg, 2014), 179.

3. Ibid., 213.

4. Susan Pinker, "An Attitude of Gratitude Brings Better Health," *Wall Street Journal*, December 19-20, 2015, National edition.

5. Ibid.

6. Watkins, *Gratitude and the Good Life*, 180, 141, 145, 122.

7. Ibid., 165.

8. Ibid., 179.

9. Ibid., 17

10. Ibid., 18.

11. Ibid., 81.

12. Pema Chodran, *Start Where You Are* (Boston: Shambhala Publications, Inc., 1994), 56.

13. Ibid.

14. Wendy Lueng, "The Science of Gratitude: As We Age, Our Brains Get Better at Being Thankful," *Toronto Globe and Mail*, October 11, 2015, International edition.

15. Ibid.

16. Pinker, *Wall Street Journal*, December 19-20, 2015.

17. Arrien, *The Second Half of Life*, 78.

18. Rumi as quoted in Ibid.

19. Richmond, *Aging as a Spiritual Practice*, 152.

20. Charlotte Berney, *Fundamentals of Hawaiian Mysticism* (Freedom, California: The Crossing Press, Inc., 2000), 18.

21. Ibid., 78.

22. Ibid.

23. Ibid., 52.

CHAPTER 14

1. Jake Curtis, "Ranking the 10 Most Iconic Moments in Wimbledon History," Bleacher Report, July 8, 2015, accessed August 2020, https://bleacherreport.com/articles/2514250-ranking-the-10-most-iconic-moments-in-wimbledon-history

2. Amanda Bennett, "Where Death Doesn't Mean

Goodbye . . .", *National Geographic*, April 2016, 61.

3. Ibid., 60.
4. Ibid., 59.
5. Ibid.
6. Ibid.
7. Ibid., 64.
8. Kastenbaum, *The Psychology of Death*, 4.
9. Ibid., 101.
10. Ibid., 98.
11. Sam Keen, foreword to *The Denial of Death*, by Ernest Becker (New York: Free Press Paperbacks, 1997), xii.
12. Kastenbaum, *The Psychology of Death*, 98.
13. Ibid., 123.
14. Butler, *Why Survive?*, 379.
15. Kastenbaum, *The Psychology of Death*, 122.
16. Nepo, *The Book of Awakening*, 83.
17. Butler, *Why Survive?*, 379-380.
18. Rinpoche, *The Tibetan Book of Living and Dying*, 11.
19. Ibid.
20. Dr. David Sanders, Dr. Lorell Frysh, Reincarnation Workshop, Kabbalah Experience, June 3, 2016.
21. Johann Wolfgang von Goethe as quoted by Dass, *Still Here*, 155.
22. His Holiness the Dalai Lama, foreword to *The Tibetan Book of Living and Dying* by Rinpoche, ix.
23. Ibid.
24. Epicurus as quoted by Shelley Kagan, *Death*, (New Haven, Connecticut: Yale University Press, 2012), 216.
25. Kagan, *Death*, 246.
26. Ibid., 299.

27. Ibid., 363.
28. Ibid., 362.
29. Ibid., 288.

CHAPTER 15

1. George Musser, *Spooky Action at A Distance* (New York: Farrar, Straus and Giroux, 2015), 11.
2. Ibid., front flyleaf of book.
3. Ibid., 4.
4. Leo Tolstoy as quoted by Butler, *Why Survive?*, 401.
5. Weil, *Healthy Aging*, 227.
6. Ibid.
7. C. Claiborne Ray, "Science Q & A," *New York Times*, April 21, 2009.
8. Ibid.
9. Marc Freedman, *Prime Time* (New York: PublicAffairs Books, 1999), 247.
10. Ibid., 246-247.
11. Ibid., 247.
12. Arrien, *The Second Half of Life*, 36.
13. Teddy Wayne, "The End of Reflection," *New York Times*, June 12, 2016, National edition.
14. Ibid.
15. Dass, *Still Here*, 134.
16. Ibid., 135.
17. Csikszentmihalyi, *Flow*, 66.
18. Ibid., 67.
19. Richmond, *Aging as a Spiritual Practice*, 78.
20. Cruikshank, *Learning to Be Old*, 173.
21. Kabat-Zinn, *Wherever You Go, There You Are*, 11.

22. Musser, *Spooky Action at a Distance*, 112.
23. Ibid.

CHAPTER 16

1. Becky Gillan, "Top 10 Demographics & Interests Facts About Americans Age 50+" on blog.aarp.org, May 14, 2014, accessed August 2020, https://blog.aarp.org/notebook/top-10-demographics-interests-facts-about-americans-age-50
2. Dass, *Still Here*, 201.
3. Cole, "The 'Enlightened' View of Aging: Victorian Morality in a New Key" in *What Does It Mean to Grow Old?*, eds. Cole and Gadow, 129-130.
4. The Who, *The Who My Generation*, "My Generation" single written by Pete Townshend, recorded by Pete Townshend, Roger Daltry, John Entwistle for Brunswick Records, released October 29, 1965.
5. Ram Dass, *Polishing the Mirror* (Boulder, Colorado: Sounds True, Inc., 2014), 64.
6. Thomas, *What Are Old People For?*, 153.

CHAPTER 17

1. Patrick Lion, "Man Who Claims He Is The World's Oldest At Age 145 Says He Is Ready To Die. . .," mailonline, *Daily Mail*, August 27, 2016, accessed August 2020, https://www.dailymail.co.uk/news/article-3761367/Indonesian-man-claims-world-s-oldest-age-145-says-ready-die-gravestone-ready-1992.html.
2. Matt Purdy, "'The First Person to Live to 150 Has

Already Been Born,'" pri.org, August 8, 2015, accessed August 2020, https://www.pri.org/stories/2015-08-08/first-person-live-150-has-already-been-born-it-you

3. Kimberly Yam, "10 Facts That Prove Helping Others Is A Key To Achieving Happiness," huffpost, March 20, 2015, accessed August 2020, https://www.huffpost.com/entry/international-day-of-happiness-helping-_n_6905446

4. Alyson Shontell, "A 69-year-old monk who scientists call the 'world's happiest man' says the secret to being happy takes just 15 minutes a day," businessinsider.com, January 27, 2016, accessed August 2020, https://www.businessinsider.com/how-to-be-happier-according-to-matthieu-ricard-the-worlds-happiest-man-2016-1

5. Ibid.

6. Ibid.

7. David Brooks, "A Moral Bucket List," *New York Times*, April 12, 2015, National edition.

8. Ibid.

9. Freedman, *Prime Time*, 248

OUTTAKES

1. Pragito Dove, "Laughter, Tears, Silence," discovermeditation.com, 2010, accessed September 2020, https://discovermeditation.com/books-and-cds/

2. Cruikshank, *Learning to Be Old*, 170.

3. Thomas, *What Are Old People For?*, 293-294.

4. Dass, *Polishing the Mirror*, xxvii.

5. Florida Scott Maxwell as quoted by Cole, *The Journey of Life*, 251.

6. Rinpoche, *The Tibetan Book of Living and Dying*, 16.
7. Arthur C. Brooks, "Be Happy: Think About Your Death," *New York Times*, January 10, 2016, National edition.

Acknowledgments

A big thanks to Mom and Dad. Even though you're no longer here, I remember everything you taught me.

Thanks to Marcy Heidish, who encouraged me when I was beginning to write this book and whose enthusiasm kept me going. To Barbara Reinish, Sandy Rhodes, Barbara Englert, Nancy Branstetter, Tony Macioce, Maria Bruno, Mike Moran, David Sanders, Katie Mazerov, Mark Levy, Ryan Lesperance, Janessa Allen, and many others, I'll always be grateful for your good advice.

A singular nod to John Ed Bon Fed, my illustrator, who drew the older woman on the cover and the other illustrations inside. Your fun, irreverent personality fits right in, John.

Special thanks to my husband, Timm, who was with me every step of the way, and to my son, Tom. Both say they're my biggest fans. And to friends, acquaintances, and extended family who kept asking me when this book would be published, now you know.

CPSIA information can be obtained
at www.ICGtesting.com
Printed in the USA
FSHW012103221021
85682FS